FELICIA CARTRIGHT

AND THE CASE OF THE
HUNGRY FIDDLER

Felicia

Joan

FELICIA CARTRIGHT

AND THE CASE OF THE
HUNGRY FIDDLER

BERNARD PALMER

Cover Artwork: Adobe Firefly

Editor: Charlene Miskimen

Aneko Press *Youth*

www.anekopress.com

Aneko Press, Life Sentence Publishing, and our logos are trademarks of Life Sentence Publishing, Inc.
203 E. Birch Street
P.O. Box 652
Abbotsford, WI 54405

JUVENILE FICTION / Religious / Christian / Action & Adventure

Paperback ISBN: 979-8-88936-302-6

eBook ISBN: 979-8-88936-303-3

10   9   8   7   6   5   4   3   2   1

Available where books are sold

CONTENTS

CHAPTER 1

A SURPRISE TRIP TO EUROPE

Mrs. Halverson shifted ponderously on the hospital bed and raised her heavy body on one elbow. Once that was accomplished, she peered intently at Felicia Cartright and Joan Bailey who were standing near the foot of her bed.

Her face was sallow and drawn, and dark crescents extended down beyond her cheekbones, evidence of the illness that had seized her. Her eyes flashed spiritedly, and her voice was firm and decisive.

"Now you two had just as well quit arguing with me," she announced evenly. "I'm simply not going to tolerate it. That's final!"

Felicia Cartright moved a step or two closer to the head of the bed, her youthful blue eyes looked with concern. "But Mrs. Halverson," she protested, "you need us now. We can't go traipsing all over Rome seeing everything while you're here in the hospital. We just can't do it."

"And why not?" she grumped testily in a way that would have frightened and dismayed both Joan and Felicia before they got to know her six weeks or so earlier. "Just what good is it going to do for me to have the two of you moping around in your hotel room or around here for a week or two? Just answer me that."

"We can keep you company," Joan Bailey put in. "You're going to get awfully lonesome up here."

"And besides," Felicia added, "we just don't feel like going around to all those places while you're so sick."

Mrs. Halverson snorted her indignation. "Sick?" she echoed. "Fiddlesticks! I may be a little under the weather, but I've never been sick a day in my life!"

A crooked smile came to Joan's lips. "The true Wellington spirit," she murmured.

Joan hadn't realized that the gray-haired lady had heard her until the older woman's eyes showed amusement.

"If you young ladies don't stop giving me trouble and do as I say, I'll show you the true Wellington spirit. Don't think I won't."

As though the talking had tired her, Mrs. Halverson sagged slowly back onto her pillow and closed her eyes. For the space of a minute or two, she breathed so evenly the girls thought she was asleep.

They just looked at one another.

After a time, she opened her eyes.

"Do you feel all right?" Felicia asked.

"Feel all right? Who could feel all right cooped

up in this–this bed with a perfectly wonderful view of the ceiling?"

"Is there something we can get for you?"

Mrs. Halverson's gruff exterior softened. "Not a thing." She smiled with a warmth Felicia and Joan both had come to recognize and love. "And I appreciate you girls wanting to stay here with me. I've sent word to my nephew to have that little Italian girl at your hotel tomorrow morning at nine. I insist that you see the sights of Rome – or as many of them as you can before that doctor comes to his senses and lets me out of here."

"We'll go sightseeing tomorrow," Joan said, "if that's what you want us to do."

"You'll go sight-seeing tomorrow and every other day I'm locked up in this–this jail of a hospital. Now don't give me any more back talk. I'm tired."

* * *

Mrs. Halverson was one of those loyal Wellington grads who always came back at homecoming and could be counted on to help raise funds or take a few lonely girls into her home on weekends. So it was not at all surprising to Miss Duncan or anyone else when she showed up on the campus one afternoon and announced that she wanted two girls to accompany her on a trip to Europe.

She went lumbering up to the room Felicia

Cartright and Joan Bailey shared and waited for them to return.

"There's somebody in your room," one of the girls told them when she met them in the hall.

"Miss Duncan?" Joan asked. "What have I done now?"

"Miss Duncan doesn't come to your room when you've done something you shouldn't," Felicia countered. "You go to Miss Duncan."

They quickened their pace. "I should know that," Joan said. "It's happened often enough."

They both recognized Mrs. Halverson at once and greeted her warmly.

She outlined the purpose of her visit bluntly. "I told Miss Duncan that I wanted two girls with spirit and life – two girls who have the old Wellington spirit. She didn't hesitate to recommend you two."

Mrs. Halverson shifted her gaze from one to the other. "I've done a little private investigating on my own, and the information I got in that way agreed with Miss Duncan's appraisal," she said. "If there is anything I can't stand, it's prissy characters who spend most of their time looking at themselves in a mirror – who would probably faint dead away at the sight of a mouse."

"Now wait a minute," Joan broke in. "Neither Felicia nor I go for that mirror routine, but to tell you the truth, Mrs. Halverson, mice and I aren't on good speaking terms."

Mrs. Halverson chuckled until her cheeks quivered.

"I know what you mean," she said. "I've been trying to become used to those pesky little creatures myself, but I haven't been able to do it in almost sixty years."

She paused and looked from one to the other significantly. "Well, answer me. What are you two going to do? Are you going to go along or aren't you?"

Felicia Cartright's eyes widened. For the first time, she began to realize that Mrs. Halverson was actually offering to take them with her. Still, it seemed almost unbelievable. "You–you mean that you want us to go to Europe with you?" she asked.

Mrs. Halverson's twinkling eyes belied the edge in her voice. "My dear, would I have come tramping up two flights and have gone into all this if I hadn't wanted you to go with me?"

So it had been decided that Felicia Cartright and Joan Bailey would accompany the wealthy Mrs. Halverson on her trip abroad.

There were envious stares from the other girls and a stern lecture from Miss Duncan about the way Wellington girls should conduct themselves in the society in which Mrs. Halverson traveled. The week after school was dismissed for the summer, Felicia and Joan were swept off to Europe by jet.

The trip had been a happy one from the first night they left the Boston airport.

Mrs. Halverson was gray-haired and given to touches of arthritis that made it necessary for her to walk with a cane, but she was sharp-eyed, inquisitive, and seemingly tireless. In London, she insisted on walking from the Charing Cross Hotel, where they stayed, down to Buckingham Palace to watch the changing of the guard.

She had struck out vigorously a pace or two ahead of Felicia and Joan under the Admiralty Arch and along the street past Clarence House and the Palace fence. She walked the girls along famous Fleet Street to St. John's Cathedral, along the Thames to Scott's sailing vessel, *Discoverer*, and back again. She led them to Westminster Abbey, London Tower, and the oldest church in the city, St. Barth's. She was alert, cheerful, and ready for more.

"When I told the travel agent I was going to take someone along with me," she confided to Felicia and Joan one night, "he suggested that I get someone nearer my own age to accompany me. Thought I would like that better."

She lifted her head and looked directly at them, her eyes flashing. "But I said, 'Young man, I don't care to take someone along who is as old as I am. I want someone who can keep up with me.'"

And it had been a fast pace through Scotland, Holland, Germany, and down into Switzerland. It was no surprise that when they got to Rome, Mrs. Halverson became sick. They had come to the Eternal City to visit her nephew, Dick Turner, employed at the American Embassy. He had started to show them around Rome when the pain in Mrs. Halverson's stomach became so unbearable she could not hide it. They took her to the hospital where the doctor pronounced it a gall attack.

"You'll only have to stay in the hospital a few days," he informed her in English.

"Stay in the hospital?" she exploded indignantly. "I refuse. I positively refuse. I have never been in the hospital in my life."

"Now Auntie," her nephew said.

"Don't you 'Auntie' me. I am not going to stay in the hospital!"

She fumed, snorted, then she went. She responded to treatment, but the doctor refused to release her until she was completely well.

"It doesn't look as though I'm ever going to get out of here," she said, "so I told Dick to engage that young Italian girl to guide you."

"But we're going to get you out of here before long, Mrs. Halverson," Joan told her, "if I have to smuggle you out in my purse."

The woman's grin widened. "The true Wellington spirit," she said.

They said goodbye and were at the door when she called them back. "Oh, yes," she said, "I almost forgot. Dick said that I should warn you to be very careful. There are a good many pickpockets and thieves around Rome at this time of year."

"We were warned about that before," Felicia told her. "We'll be careful."

"You'll take care of yourselves," Mrs. Halverson said. "I have no fear of that. I told Dick that if any thief were brash enough to tackle a girl from Wellington, he deserved just what he'd get."

Felicia and Joan went out into the still of the night together, hailed a cab, and gave the name of the hotel where they were staying. The driver's brow furrowed as he considered their American pronunciation. Then he smiled, nodded his head vigorously, and drove off.

"I never know whether I've finally gotten through to them," Joan said, "or whether they just give up and decide they'll pick out some place on their own to take us."

When they got back to the hotel, the man at the desk smiled pleasantly. "It is too bad, *Signorine,* that you have miss your Italian friend."

They stopped and went over to the desk. "Italian friend?" Felicia asked. "Who was that?"

"He do not leave name, but you know him. He ask all about the *signorine* from America. He ask how long you have stay – when you plan to leave. He say it is so long since he see you. He must see you before you leave Rome."

"But we don't know anyone here," Joan said.

"Maybe it was Mr. Turner," Felicia suggested.

"He might have come and asked about us."

"But why? We just saw him this morning. He knows that we'll be here for some time."

The clerk's eyes seemed to light when Joan released that bit of information, but the look faded, and he glanced at them uneasily.

"What did he look like?" Felicia insisted.

"I–I do not remember so well, *Signorina*. I have not really look at him." Suddenly he got very busy. "If he comes, I will get name," he added.

The girls remained at the desk looking at the clerk.

"*Signor,*" Joan said.

He looked up. "Really, *Signorina* Bailey, I am very busy." He turned his back deliberately.

"Well, now," Joan said to Felicia when they were in their room, "what do you make of that?"

Felicia took off her jacket. "I've never seen such a change come over a person so quickly," she said. "He was as friendly as could be until we started asking questions. Then he froze."

"It certainly gave me a funny feeling," Joan answered, "but it probably isn't anything."

"Maybe not." Felicia moved to the window and looked out on the darkened street below. "But just the same," she concluded, "I'm glad we're up here instead of out on the street. I don't like the idea of having a strange man inquiring about us."

"Neither do I," Joan said. "I don't like it at all."

Felicia turned her back to the window. "What do you suppose he wanted?"

CHAPTER 2

THE MAN WITH A VIOLIN

The following day broke warm and sunny, and Felicia Cartright and Joan Bailey almost forgot the incident that had taken place in the hotel lobby the night before.

"We're going to have to hurry," Joan said with a quick glance at her watch, "if we are going to finish breakfast before our guide is to arrive at nine o'clock."

Felicia moved to the mirror, took a quick look to be sure her hair was in place, and moved toward the door.

"Wasn't Mrs. Halverson a dear to insist that we go out sightseeing while she's in the hospital?" she asked. "She tries so hard to make us think she's gruff and hard-boiled, but she's as kind, gentle, and considerate as anyone I know."

Mrs. Halverson's nephew, Dick Turner, was waiting for them in the lobby on a sofa near the stairway.

Beside him sat an attractive, olive-skinned girl about their own age or slightly younger.

"I was just going to call for you," he said, getting to his feet. "This is Claudia Proveddi. You'll be seeing a lot of her the next few days. She's going to be guiding for you."

"We're so glad to meet you."

Claudia shook hands with them warmly. She was a trim, sweet-faced young woman a little shorter than Felicia. Her dark eyes seemed to dominate her entire being. They were large, soft, and smiling.

"Auntie said I should have Claudia come over here and introduce herself to you this morning," Mr. Turner continued, "but I decided to bring her to the hotel and introduce her to you myself on my way to work."

"Thank you," Joan answered.

He stood there for a moment or two as though deciding whether to speak or not. Both girls sensed his indecision. "By the way," he said after a time, "you girls are getting popular."

"What do you mean?" Felicia asked him.

"We had a phone call about you at the embassy late yesterday afternoon."

The color left her cheeks.

"It isn't anything to be alarmed about," he went on. "The caller said he was very anxious to get in touch with you girls, and he wanted to know where you were staying and how long you would be in Rome.

Apparently, he knows that you are accompanying my aunt and that she is in the hospital for a few days."

"What happened then?" Joan asked.

"That's the strange thing," the embassy official said. "When I asked his name, he hung up."

He smiled as he noticed the consternation in the girls' eyes.

"It isn't anything to be so upset about," he told them. "The chances are the guy is just someone who is a long way from home and knew someone with a name like one of yours or is from the same hometown or something of the sort."

"Was he an American?" Joan asked. "Did he speak English with an accent?"

Mr. Turner's lips made a firm, straight line, and he tugged the lobe of his ear. "Come to think of it," he answered, "I was busy when he called and didn't notice."

He guided the girls toward the dining room. "If we hurry," he said, "I can have breakfast with you before I have to report at the office."

That, as far as he was concerned, ended the matter. He talked with them of the things they would be doing that day and did not mention the phone call again.

It took longer for them to be served than usual, so Mr. Turner had to hurry his breakfast in order to get to the embassy on time.

"I've got to run," he said, glancing at his watch

and pushing back from the table. "Claudia will take good care of you."

She smiled at him.

"Greet Mrs. Halverson for us when you see her," Felicia called after him as he walked away.

"I'll do that."

"And tell her that we'll be praying she'll be able to join us before long," Joan added.

Felicia, who happened to be glancing at their young guide when Joan spoke, caught a strange look in the girl's dark eyes. For a moment, the silence was strained.

Not until after the waiter had brought them another cup of coffee did Claudia Proveddi direct her attention to the two Americans she was to accompany on a tour of the city for the next few days.

"I hope I'll be able to show you what you want to see during your stay in Rome," she began hesitantly.

"I thought you were a regular guide," Joan told her.

Claudia laughed nervously. "Oh, no. This is the first time I have ever done anything like this. I'm actually a typist and do some of the extra work at the American Embassy. Mr. Turner knew I wasn't working for a week or so, and he called me to help you."

"You know the places we'd like to see," Joan continued. "We haven't seen anything here, so whatever you decide to show us will be interesting."

Claudia frowned and consulted the guidebook

she had picked up at a nearby kiosk on the way to the hotel.

"But there is so much to see here in Rome that I hardly know where to start," she said, looking from one to the other. "What would you like to see first? Ruins? Old churches?"

Felicia was the first to reply. "I want to see it all," she said, "or as much as we can; but I'd like to start with the Colosseum, the Catacombs, and places like that which figure so much in the early history of Christianity. I'm sure that Joan feels the same way."

"Oh, I do," Joan Bailey put in quickly. "I was thinking when we had our Bible reading last night that it doesn't seem possible that we are actually where Paul preached and was imprisoned, where so many of the first century Christians lost their lives because of their faith in and devotion to Jesus Christ."

Felicia turned to their Italian guide. "It must be wonderful to live in a place like this where you are constantly reminded of the sacrifices early Christians made."

Claudia's eyes looked cold. "I wouldn't know," she retorted. "I've never thought much about it."

She stood, then picked up the check. "We had better be going," she said. "We'll not get to see too much today. It's already after nine o'clock."

Claudia took them to the Colosseum first, great ruins that are still one of the wonders of the world. She stopped by the Forum since it was close and then took them to the church where Luther was going up the marble staircase on his knees when he saw, for the first time, that salvation was the gift of grace and was by faith and not by works.

"This is something I've never been able to understand," she said, gesturing toward the staircase with her hand. "It hardly seems possible that people in this modern age would still go up those stairs in the way Luther did. But they do it."

"The Bible doesn't teach it," Felicia told her. "The Bible says, *For by grace are ye saved through faith; and that not of yourselves: it is the gift of God: Not of works, lest any man should boast.*"

"I get along very well without religion," Claudia said coldly. "So do my family and friends." With that she consulted her guidebook and hailed a cab. "We will go and see the Appian Way now," she said. "The Catacombs we will save until later."

She withdrew to the far corner of the taxi where she sat in silence. It was half an hour or more before she talked with the girls again, and then guardedly, as if to keep them from talking about spiritual things.

After a day of sightseeing, they had dinner at a little cafe a block or so from the hotel. When they had finished, they walked along the dimly lighted street.

"It was so good to have you showing us around today, Claudia," Joan said. "We both enjoyed it a great deal."

"I enjoyed it too," she replied. "It has been years since I have visited some of those places myself."

They were talking pleasantly when a gaunt, angular stranger stepped out of the darkness and approached them.

"*Signorina,*" he said in broken English. "Please, one moment! I must talk with you! Please!" There was a note of desperation in his voice.

Joan Bailey, Felicia Cartright, and Claudia Proveddi stopped involuntarily and turned to stare at him.

The man was wearing trousers several sizes too large for him around the middle and held up by a length of cord. His wrinkled suit coat was ragged at the cuffs, and one elbow had broken through.

It was his face that haunted Felicia and Joan. His black eyes were sharp and piercing, and his cheeks were hollow. One hand was in his pocket and the other that clutched the violin case under his arm was very thin.

"W-w-what do you want?" Joan managed. Fright gripped her, and she took half a step backward without realizing it.

His crooked smile revealed a few brown snags for teeth.

"I would talk with you, Signorine," he repeated.

CHAPTER 3

THE STRANGER
APPEARS AGAIN

F elicia Cartright and Joan Bailey stared at the
stranger who stood before them.

"Come," Claudia said. She spoke sharply to the
man in Italian, but he paid no attention.

"*Signorina,*" he said, shifting his gaze from Joan
to Felicia and back again. "Please!"

"Who are you?" Joan demanded, her voice rising,
"and what do you want?"

"I am Eduardo Olivetti," he answered.

"Come on," Claudia said, taking Joan by the arm.
"You shouldn't be standing here talking with him.
He's a beggar."

"But no, *Signorina*" he answered. His voice was
mild enough, but his eyes showed anger. "Poor, yes,
but beggar? No! I have the desire to talk with the
Signorine about the violin."

He tapped the case under his arm.

"We aren't interested in your violin!" Claudia said angrily. "Go on and leave us alone!"

He brushed her aside with a glance. "Please?" His eyes sought Felicia's.

"I'm sorry." She pushed past him and went on to the hotel, Joan and Claudia at her side.

Once in the hotel lobby, their youthful guide apologized for what had happened in the street.

"I am sorry something like that had to happen," she said. "Most of the people in Rome are not like that, but there are a few who want to take advantage of guests from America and other countries."

"I know," Felicia said. "We have people like that in America too. I think every country has them."

Claudia offered her hand.

"Good night," she said. "I will see you tomorrow morning."

Once in their room, Joan locked their door and tried it to see that it was secured.

"That was wonderful!" she exclaimed, taking off her jacket. "One of the most interesting days we've had since we left home. I only wish Mrs. Halverson could have been with us."

Felicia was not listening. She was standing with her back to the mirror, staring across the room. Joan saw the look in her eyes.

"Don't tell me!" she said. "Let me guess! You're worrying about the man with the violin."

"Not worrying," Felicia corrected, "but I can't help thinking about him. He looked so thin and hungry." She took a deep breath. "Do you suppose he has had anything to eat today?"

"If you ask me," Joan answered, "he gives me the creeps." She went over to the window and checked it carefully.

"What are you doing?" her roommate asked.

"I just want to be sure this window is locked," she said. "If we have company, I want them to come to the door and knock."

"The trouble with you," Felicia countered, "is that you're too suspicious."

When they got up the next morning, Joan faced Felicia with mock indignation. "Do you know what you did?" she demanded. "You talked so much about that poor, hungry fiddler last night that you had me dreaming about him."

"That was just your conscience hurting you because you were cruel and heartless."

"You don't even know what I dreamed," Joan countered. "I dreamed that guy was hiding out there in the alley, and when we came by, he started to chase us. We ran and ran and ran, but we couldn't get away from him."

She shuddered. "He had a great big violin case and was going to trap us in it."

That morning when the girls left the hotel with Claudia Proveddi shortly after eight o'clock, Joan thought she caught a glimpse of the man. He was standing in a doorway just around the corner, staring in their direction. He seemed taller and darker, and there was a short, livid scar across his left cheek. Their eyes met, and his lips parted as though in recognition.

Joan's heartbeat quickened. For an instant or two, it seemed that he was going to approach them. He took half a step forward. That did it. She grasped her companions by the arm and hurried them out into the intersection.

"Joan!" Felicia exclaimed, "What's the big idea?"

It was only then that Felicia realized that Joan's hand was trembling.

"I–I thought I saw that man," she stammered.

That afternoon, the girls broke their sightseeing long enough to stop at the hospital and visit Mrs. Halverson. She tried to scold them for doing it, but it was obvious that she was pleased.

"It's a good thing you came today," she said. "I told that young doctor that I had stood enough of all his nonsense, and so he decided he had better get me out of here. He's releasing me tomorrow."

"I suppose you'll be going to your nephew's house for a few days to recuperate," Felicia volunteered.

Mrs. Halverson scowled. "I most certainly will not be going to my nephew's to recuperate," she snorted. "What do you think I've been doing in the hospital?

When I get out of here, I'm going to see the sights the same as you're doing."

Felicia's smile widened. "It's so good to see you feeling better," she said. "Joan and I have been praying for you."

Mrs. Halverson's stern face softened. "I knew you were." She reached out and picked up her own Bible which was on the stand beside the bed. "But this time in the hospital hasn't been wasted. It's been a wonderful period of communion with the Lord. It's been very precious to me."

Claudia Proveddi squirmed uncomfortably.

Mrs. Halverson noticed it. "Now what's the matter with you?" she demanded.

The young Italian woman flushed scarlet but did not reply.

Then understanding flooded the older woman's eyes. "You are embarrassed by the way we talk about the Lord, aren't you?" she asked. There was a gentleness in her voice that Felicia didn't believe possible. "My dear, don't be embarrassed. Christ loved us so much that He died on the cross to save us from our sin – even a short-tempered old lady like me."

She paused for a minute or two. "Christ died to save you, too, Claudia," she concluded. "That is, from the results of sin."

The guide looked up, her pretty, young face twisted with anger and defiance. "I can live my own life the way I want to without help from religion or anything else."

"That's what I used to think," Felicia said. "But I soon found that the Bible is right when it says that we have to serve either God or Satan. One or the other is going to be master."

Her words struck deeply into Claudia's heart. That was apparent.

The nurse came in just then and informed them that visiting hours were over.

"I'm going to be seeing you girls tomorrow," Mrs. Halverson called after them. "Don't see everything before I join you."

"As long as Mrs. Halverson is going to be out of the hospital tomorrow," Felicia said when they reached the sidewalk, "why don't we do some shopping this afternoon and wait until she can be with us to finish sightseeing?"

"Sounds like a good idea," Joan said.

Claudia took them to a number of little shops on side streets. They bought two or three not too expensive cameos and several small gifts. The afternoon flew, and by the time they left the last shop, the shadows were already beginning to lengthen.

"I'm hungry," Joan said.

"So am I." Felicia turned to their guide. "I just loved that little cafe we ate in last night. Could we go there for dinner?"

"If you like."

They hailed a cab and went to the restaurant a block and a half from the hotel. When they finished eating, Claudia wanted to go with them to their room, but they insisted on going alone.

"You've been taking us around all day," Felicia said, "and I know you're tired."

"It won't take but a few minutes to go over to the hotel with you," the guide said.

"We can get to the hotel without any trouble," Joan put in. "Besides, it's such a lovely evening we might walk around for a little while."

"If you think it will be all right," Claudia agreed reluctantly.

She left them, and they sauntered slowly along the street in the darkness.

"It's really hard to believe that we're actually in Rome where the early Christians were martyred," Felicia said.

Joan Bailey nodded. "And where Paul was imprisoned."

They crossed the street and paused to look in a store window.

"What do you think about Claudia?" Felicia asked after a time.

"She seems like a sweet girl."

"But she is indifferent to the things of God," she added. "She bothers me."

"Remember how I used to be when you first started talking with me about the Savior?" Joan asked. "I acted the same way or worse. I think it was because I was so terribly convicted of the sin in my life. I knew that things weren't right in my life. I knew that I was a sinner and was lost, but at the same time I was determined that I was going to run my own life."

They finished looking in the window and walked on in the warm evening air. They were talking as they walked and neared the hotel without realizing exactly where they were. They were both startled and almost cried out when the tall, poorly dressed stranger stepped out suddenly to block their way.

Joan almost turned and fled.

"*Signorina* Bailey," he said, "don't run! I have wait to talk to you!"

Joan's mouth sagged. "H-h-how did you know my name?" she blurted.

CHAPTER 4

A VIOLIN ON LOAN

"**H**ow did you know my name?" Joan Bailey demanded once more.

The corners of his mouth twitched, and a strange, trapped look came to his eyes. "I have hear your friends speak of you," he said, nodding toward Felicia.

This time it was Felicia Cartright who was anxious to go on. She tightened her grip on Joan's arm and started to push past him. But he moved to block the way.

"You remember me, don't you?" he asked. "Eduardo Olivetti?"

"Really, Mr. Olivetti," she said, her voice trembling in spite of her efforts to control it, "we have to hurry."

"One moment!" There was a deep pleading in his voice. "Please! I must talk with you!"

For a minute, Felicia and Joan remained motionless,

looking up into the sharp, piercing eyes of the stranger who stood before them.

"If you don't let us pass," Joan informed him, "we are going to call the police!"

He glanced about quickly in a moment of wild desperation. "Please, *Signorina* Bailey," he said. "Please! Do not call the police. Listen to Eduardo!"

He shifted the violin from one arm to the other as though making ready to dash away at any moment. "Please! I will not hurt you! I wish only to talk to you!"

Felicia was the one who yielded first. "If you're going to talk," she said, "you'll have to talk fast. We'll only stay and talk with you for a minute or two."

"Oh, thank you, *Signorina*."

"What is it you want?" Joan asked.

He took a deep breath and launched into his story quickly. "I–I would not bother you like this," he said, "but there is no money, and I am so hungry. My family are so hungry."

Felicia caught her breath. "Oh, that's too bad," she exclaimed. "Is there anything we can do to help?"

"You are kind, *Signorina*. I knew if you listen, you will understand." He took the violin from under his arm and held it out to her. "It is not that I wish to sell this to you. It is my most prize owning. You loan me some money, no? You take the violin to be sure I come back and give you your money."

Her gaze dropped to the battered violin case.

"See," he said, "here is the violin." He opened the case and let them peek inside.

"You want us to take your violin and hold it as security for a loan?" Felicia asked.

He nodded. "That is how you say it. Give as security for a loan?" he asked. "That is it. But it is not for me. It is not for Eduardo Olivetti that I do this. It is not even for my wife, maybe. But the children – my little bambinos – they are so little."

His voice tremored as though he was about to cry. "Every day they say to me, 'Papa, when you buy the bread? When are you bringing home the spaghett'?'"

He shrugged his shoulders. "What can I tell them? I have no job – no money."

Joan saw that Felicia's eyes were soft and luminous. "Take it easy, Felicia," she whispered under her breath. "This sounds like a big story to me."

"But no!" Eduardo protested. "It is not a big story. It is true! The little bambinos are so hungry."

Felicia's heart melted.

"Are you sure that your children will get the benefit of this money if we do let you have it?" she asked.

"But of course!" he exclaimed. The light in his dark eyes brightened. "Why else would a man like me – a man like Eduardo Olivetti – come and plead with you?"

He inched forward and lowered his voice. "I have tell no one else this, but my brother, he send me some money from America. He is rich man there. It come in three – four days – it come soon in the mail. So soon as I get it, I give it to you."

"I–I don't know," she said uncertainly.

"You will have save my children's lives!"

"Don't believe him, Felicia," Joan whispered in an undertone. "It sounds like a story. He thinks we're a soft touch."

Felicia looked into her purse. "I know that," she said, "but there's a chance that he's telling us the truth. There's a good chance that he actually has a family and is getting money from America soon."

She took out her wallet and held it.

"I don't have very much money," she said, "but I could let you have a little. Would fifty dollars help?"

"Fifty dollar!" Eduardo Olivetti's eyes gleamed. "Fifty dollar! You have save my life! You are my friend. You are the friend of my wife and my little bambinos! I could kiss you a thousand times, *Signorina!*"

Felicia retreated. "Y-y-you needn't bother." She took a bill from her purse and handed it to him.

He glanced at it almost indifferently and stuffed it into his pocket. "You will take care of my violin?" he asked. "You will watch so nothing happen to it?"

"We'll take care of it," Felicia assured him. "And we'll expect you to pick it up just as soon as you get the letter from your brother."

He nodded and would have left immediately, but she stopped him. "Where do you live, Mr. Olivetti?"

Felicia asked. "I should know in case we have to get in touch with you."

He hesitated as though there was a protest on his lips, but Felicia realized she must have been mistaken. He fished a stub of pencil from his pocket and began to write on a scrap of paper.

"My address," he said. "But you have no need for it. As soon as my money comes, I will come to you and get the violin."

With that, he was gone.

Felicia watched until he disappeared from view. The violin was still in her arms. Joan turned to her, amusement in her eyes.

"I knew that you have been wanting to get a souvenir from Rome to take back with you," she said, "but I certainly didn't know you were going to buy a violin. When do you start taking lessons?"

She made a face at her companion and then colored. "I didn't buy a violin, Joan," she countered, "and you know it. I just loaned Mr. Olivetti the money until he gets a check from his American brother."

"Don't hold your breath until it comes," Joan answered laconically. "That's one of the oldest dodges in the world. He got you to feeling so sorry that you couldn't wait to let him take your money."

"The trouble with you," Felicia said, "is that you don't have any confidence in human nature."

"And the trouble with you is that you believe everything anyone tells you."

They went into the hotel together and up to their room where Felicia opened the case and took out the violin. "It's beautiful, isn't it?" she said.

Joan sniffed it. "It smells a little musty to me. He's probably had it buried somewhere."

Felicia took it and put it back. "If you're going to make fun of it, I'm going to put it away and not let you look at it anymore." She closed the case.

"What you should do," her roommate continued, "is take that violin back to Wellington with you. That would certainly make a hit with Miss Duncan. She always says that the well-rounded, Wellington-educated young lady should have a musical instrument."

Her smile deepened. "Of course, it would help if you knew how to play the scale or something, Felicia, but it is sort of pretty – if it weren't a little on the old side."

"I can always sell it if Olivetti doesn't come back."

Joan burst into laughter. "It's probably worth all of ten euros," she said. "And you probably wouldn't be able to get half that. You just bought yourself a violin, that's all. He's probably got the attic full of others just like it."

"At any rate," the Cartright girl said defensively, "I know that I have helped him to get some food for his children – even though I did buy a violin."

Joan crossed the room, shaking her head. "You are naive if you believed that story," she said. "More naive than I thought you were. He probably doesn't have any children – or a wife either, for that matter."

Felicia pushed the violin case under the bed. "Well," she said, "I've got his address. We can drive by there tomorrow and see if he has a wife or not."

"It'll just make you feel bad, but if you want to do it, it'll be fine with me. I'd like to see where this *Signor* Eduardo Olivetti lives. He's probably got a beautiful villa he's paid for by selling violins to Americans who feel sorry for him."

They finished their evening devotions before either of them said anything more about Eduardo Olivetti.

"You know," Felicia said, "there was something curious about him."

Joan grinned impishly. "You're talking about the violin salesman, no doubt."

Felicia ignored the jibe. "He's ragged and looks as though he hasn't eaten in a long time," she said. "But did you notice how well he speaks English?"

"Maybe he spent some time in America."

"I suppose that's possible," she said, "but he does sound educated."

She expelled her breath slowly. "There's some sort of a mystery about him."

"I think the mystery is about you," Joan countered. "How you are so gullible as to fall for every hard luck story anyone throws at you."

Felicia picked up a pillow and threw it at Joan, who ducked easily.

The following morning, they had a call from the hospital that Mrs. Halverson was being discharged.

"We'll be there in an hour," Joan told the nurse who called.

She had just hung up when the phone rang, and Claudia Proveddi was in the lobby waiting for them.

"We are slow getting around this morning," Joan said.

At the door, Felicia paused. "Don't say anything to Mrs. Halverson or Claudia about the violin, shall we?" she asked, "at least for now?"

Joan nodded. "I won't say anything," she promised. "I'll think plenty, but I won't say anything."

In the lobby, Felicia handed the slip of paper to their guide.

"Do you suppose you could take us by this place on the way to the hospital, Claudia?" she asked, trying hard to sound as though it were nothing of great importance.

Claudia's brow crinkled. "If you like," she said quizzically.

"If it isn't too far out of the way."

"Oh, no," the Italian girl answered, "It isn't more than a few blocks out of the way."

They hailed a cab and got in. "Now," Felicia whispered to Joan, "we'll soon find out whether the guy with the violin is lying to us about having a wife and family."

The driver made two or three sharp turns, sped

up a narrow, twisting street, and turned again, this time toward an old ruin. Claudia spoke to him, and he pulled over to the curb and stopped.

"Well," she said, "did you wish to get out?"

The question in Felicia's eyes grew. "But this is the Forum," she protested. "We have no reason to want to stop here."

"I beg your pardon." There was a trace of ice in her voice. "But you told me you wanted to stop at the address you gave me on the paper."

Slowly the truth seeped through Felicia's consciousness.

"You mean this is the address on the paper?" she asked.

"That's right."

"I–I'm sorry," Felicia apologized, coloring. "I don't care to stop here after all."

Joan, who was sitting on the other side of her, almost exploded as she fought to keep laughter down.

CHAPTER 5

ITALIAN HOSPITALITY

Claudia Proveddi took Joan Bailey and Felicia Cartright to the hospital where Mrs. Halverson was waiting impatiently.

"It wasn't that I minded staying here so much," she grumped, "but I was afraid that young whippersnapper of a doctor would change his mind and put me to bed again."

When Felicia and Joan went to help her down the steps, she shook them off.

"I can still navigate on my own two pins," she said. "As long as I can, I'd like to do it, if it's all the same to you."

"I'm sorry we were so late in getting here," Felicia told her when they got into the cab. "We had a little errand to do on the way, and it took longer than we thought it would."

"As a matter of fact," Joan added, "we were going

to look up an address that Felicia had, but when we got there, it turned out to be the Forum."

"That's interesting," Mrs. Halverson said, her interest quickening. "Where would you be getting an address here in Rome, Felicia? Sounds mysterious."

"It isn't," she replied. "At least not very. But it's a long story."

For a time, a hurt look came to the older woman's eyes. Felicia leaned forward impulsively.

"We'll tell you all about it when we get to the hotel."

Mrs. Halverson surveyed her critically. Her left eyelid dropped in a quick, understanding wink.

Felicia and Joan wanted to return to the hotel so Mrs. Halverson could rest, but she would have none of it.

"You can go back to the hotel if you want to," she announced decisively. "I'm going to see something this afternoon. You remember I've been in that hospital room almost since the hour we hit town. I haven't seen a thing."

"There's always tomorrow," Felicia said.

"But why waste a perfectly good afternoon like we have today?" Mrs. Halverson asked her. "No siree. I'm going to see something before you get me to the hotel. That's all there is to it."

Although Mrs. Halverson's determination was as strong as ever, even she had to admit that her stay in the hospital had weakened her. They made a start through St. Peter's Cathedral but turned back before they had covered a small corner.

"There's no use in denying it any longer," the gray-haired woman said, puffing. "I must be getting old. All I want to do is find a nice comfortable rocking chair and sit down with my feet on a stool."

"I don't think either of us could have done half as well as you have this afternoon," Felicia said. "After all, you just got out of the hospital today."

"That doctor!" Mrs. Halverson exclaimed. "I still get mad when I think of it! Imagine him putting me to bed!"

When they got back to the hotel where they had secured an adjoining room for Mrs. Halverson, Felicia told her what had taken place and showed her the violin.

"Can't say that I blame you for being taken in that way," she said, "but I'm like Joan. I think the guy saw you coming and figured you for a soft touch. People like that are very clever in the way they can tell who is apt to fall for a good sob story."

She handed the violin back to Felicia who returned it to the case and put it back under the bed. "What makes me so angry," she said, "is that he took advantage of me."

"Why don't you tell Claudia about it?" Mrs. Halverson suggested. "She might be able to help you get your money back."

The following morning Felicia did just that. Claudia

was indignant. "I don't know why they allow people like that to go free!" she exclaimed. "They are embarrassing to those of us who are decent and law-abiding, and they give the whole country a bad name."

"I wouldn't have said anything about it," Felicia continued, "but I thought you might be able to help me get my money back."

Claudia thought for a moment. "The problem would be in finding the man and identifying him, I suppose."

"We wouldn't have any trouble in identifying him," Joan broke in. "I think we'd both know him if we ever saw him again."

"That's right," the Italian girl replied, "and for that matter, I suppose I would recognize him myself if I ever saw him again."

"Felicia could go to the police, couldn't she?" Mrs. Halverson suggested.

Claudia's eyes narrowed. "You could go to the police station," she said, "and swear out a warrant for Eduardo Olivetti, and if they can find him, they'll arrest him and bring him in. You'd have to identify him and appear in court against him."

Felicia Cartright breathed deeply.

"I suppose you're hesitating because you're thinking about his wife and children," Joan taunted good-naturedly.

Felicia made a face at her. "Actually, it sounds as though it's more trouble than it's worth. I think I'll just let it go and remember never to fall for a story like that again."

"Until the next time."

They left the hotel, and, at Mrs. Halverson's suggestion, went to the open market.

There were little stands of vegetables and meat and fruit around an entire city block. Scattered among them were racks of yard and leather goods, suitcases, clothes, and almost anything a person might want to buy. Each stand owner was calling out his wares in a loud voice to add to the confusion.

Mrs. Halverson's bout with a tricky gall bladder was all but forgotten as she went from one stand to another, examining the fruit and vegetables with a practiced eye.

"Good quality," she told the girls, "and good prices, too. Do you shop here, Claudia?"

"We live not far from here," the young guide told her. "Mama comes here often to buy for the family."

Mrs. Halverson nodded her approval.

Felicia Cartright had completely forgotten all the strange things that had happened since they arrived in Rome. She forgot them, that is, until she realized they were being followed. At first, she thought it just a coincidence that the squat, evil-faced little man was moving from one stand to the next, thirty paces or so behind them. Then she noticed that whenever they moved, he moved, even though he had to walk away from a salesperson to do so. When they stopped, he stopped, as casually as though he had nothing else to do other than to wander from stand to stand. On one occasion, their eyes met, and she was sure that he leered at her.

Felicia sidled over to Joan and Claudia, her face pale and moist with perspiration. She whispered to them.

"Don't say anything to Mrs. Halverson," she said, "but we're being followed."

"You must be mistaken," Claudia countered evenly. "That sort of thing wouldn't happen in the middle of the day."

"I'm positive. Don't be too obvious about it, but just watch."

Joan glanced back and squeezed her roommate's arm tightly. "I–I saw him!" she managed.

Claudia saw him, too. Her expression did not change, but she was disturbed. Felicia read it in her eyes. "I know what we'll do," she said. "We're not far from where my family lives, and I'd like to have you meet them. Won't you come home with me for lunch?"

Mrs. Halverson was elated with the prospect of getting into the Proveddi home. "That's the most exciting thing you could have thought of," she said.

They left the market abruptly and cut across the street and around the corner to the apartment house where Claudia lived with her family. The girls were walking quite rapidly, and Mrs. Halverson did her best to keep up. It wasn't long, however, until she began to puff laboriously and drop back. Felicia noticed it and stopped.

"We'll have to slow down a little, girls," she said.

"I thought I could keep up," Mrs. Halverson said, "but staying in that hospital took more out of me than I realized. I should never have let that young whippersnapper put me in bed. That's what's wrong. It took all my strength."

They stood on the street for a moment or two, talking, while they waited for her to rest. It was then that Felicia chanced to look back and caught a glimpse of the stranger. He was loitering at a bus stop half a block away.

He was the same man! She was sure of it! He had the same slouch to his shoulders – the same studied carelessness in his manner.

Her eyes met Joan's fearfully.

Joan looked back, too, startled at the sight of him.

"If you're looking at that man who's following us," Mrs. Halverson said laconically, "he's been back there for an hour."

The girls stared at her. "How did you know he is following us?"

"How did I know he was there?" she asked, her voice rising indignantly. "I saw him. How else would I know he was following? You thought you were going to hide it from me."

"We didn't want to worry you," Joan told her.

Mrs. Halverson managed a broad smile. "That's

kind of you, my dear," she answered, "but I've been trusting the Lord for almost twice as many years as you are old. I don't fret about things like that."

She paused. "Besides, a Wellington girl is trained to cope with any situation."

"Just the same," Felicia said, "I think we'd better be on our way. It makes me uncomfortable just knowing he's back there."

The older woman looked at him curiously. "I wonder what he wants," she said. "Why do you suppose he's following us?"

Claudia touched her on the elbow. "It is better that we go now," she said firmly.

They went into the building and up to the eighth floor by elevator to the apartment where the Proveddi family lived. Theirs was a pleasant, old-fashioned apartment with massive furniture and huge paintings on the wall.

Mr. and Mrs. Proveddi welcomed them graciously, their broad smiles crossing the language barrier. Papa Proveddi was a short, muscular individual with a receding hairline and a stomach that paunched over his belt. His face was fluid and expressive, and his eyes were alight with friendliness. Mama Proveddi was an ample, round-faced woman with her dark hair brought severely over her ears and pinned in a knot at the back. She looked older to Felicia and Joan than she probably was, but there was a youthful sparkle in her eyes.

"Mama says she is very happy to have you here for lunch," Claudia interpreted after she and her mother had a short discussion in Italian. "She says she would like to have you make yourselves at home while she finishes cooking."

Mama Proveddi excused herself after a moment or two and went to the kitchen while Papa Proveddi sat down across from them. Claudia continued to serve as interpreter.

"And what do you find the most interesting here in Rome?" Papa asked Felicia after a moment or two.

"It's been so wonderful to see the places where the early Christians were persecuted," she answered. "I don't know exactly why, but just visiting the Colosseum and the Catacombs makes me feel my own unworthiness and the strength of the love Christ has for us."

She took a deep breath and expelled it slowly. "I can't help wondering what I would have done if I had been here at that time. I–I'm afraid that I wouldn't have had the courage to stand firm. I know I couldn't have done anything like it in my own strength."

Claudia's cheeks paled, and she interpreted a sentence or two. Her papa spoke to her sharply, and she continued. When she finished, he spoke again, and she turned to Felicia. Twin spots of scarlet now appeared, one on either cheek.

"Papa said for me to tell you that I only interpreted part of what you said to him, but he made me tell him all of it. He says he does not understand what you are talking about. Religion oppresses the people. It is like a–like a–" She searched in desperation for words. "Like a thing that hangs on and steals away the strength from a man."

Felicia thought for a moment, prayerfully. "I was not talking about religion," she told him. "I was talking about being a Christian."

"There is a difference?" he asked curiously.

"Christianity is a religion," she went on, "but it is so much more than that. I think of the Hindu who worships his cow as being religious, or the African woman who sacrifices one of her twins. Christianity is a way of life."

She went on to explain the way of salvation, how a person must recognize that he is a sinner and needs a Savior, how he must believe that Christ has the power to save, and how he must put his trust in Him.

"That is what being a Christian is," she concluded.

Claudia squirmed uncomfortably as she interpreted, and her scowl deepened.

"You do make it sound different," he said, "and very interesting. It is almost something a man might put his trust in."

Claudia's face darkened. "Papa may talk that way," she said defensively, "but he has no religion. He boasts that he has not been in church since he was a boy when his mama made him go. Right after the war, he even called himself a Communist."

Before Felicia had an opportunity to reply, Claudia

got to her feet. "If you will excuse me, **I** must go and help Mama in the kitchen."

Mr. Proveddi leaned back in his chair and looked at Felicia and her companions. His lips parted, and he smiled genially. They smiled back at him.

He started to speak in Italian and checked himself. He went over to one of the pictures on the wall, pointed to it, and then to himself.

The girls and Mrs. Halverson looked at him blankly.

Then he outlined an imaginary easel with his hands, sat down before it, and began to make vigorous painting motions.

"I see now!" Joan exclaimed. "You painted the picture!"

He did not understand her words, but he understood the inflection in her voice and the smiles on their faces.

His own smile grew broader, and he nodded. At last, however, he turned his head and called over his shoulder, "Claudia. Claudia!"

She came to the door, smiling in spite of herself as he spoke to her in Italian. She entered the room uneasily and said to Mrs. Halverson and the girls, "Papa says I must come in here and sit down. He says it gets too quiet when I'm gone."

They ate soon, with much laughter and gesturing and a little talking. Claudia interpreted as best she could for them all.

So the afternoon went by. When the girls and

Mrs. Halverson finally rose to leave toward evening, it was with genuine regret.

"This has been a wonderful day," Mrs. Halverson said, taking Mama Proveddi's hand in both of hers. "May God bless you richly." She stopped for a moment or two. "I'm going to pray that God will speak to your hearts so you will all accept Him as your Savior."

The look on Mama Proveddi's face showed that Claudia had interpreted correctly. There was longing there, and tears came to her eyes. She patted Mrs. Halverson's hand with her own work-worn palms.

"Mama says, 'Thank you,'" Claudia interpreted.

"It won't be necessary for you to go all the way back to the hotel with us, Claudia," Joan said at the door. "We can get a cab and get there without any trouble."

"I can go down with you and help you get a taxi if you wish."

She rode down the elevator with them. On the main floor, Felicia looked out into the growing dusk. "Do you think that man will be waiting out there for us?" she asked uneasily.

"I should have brought my cane," Mrs. Halverson said crisply. "That's what I'll do the next time. I'll take my cane. Then just let that fat, little upstart bother us. Just let him try."

Joan studied her admiringly. "I do believe you'd wrap it around his neck," she said.

"I probably wouldn't," the gray-haired woman

admitted, "I'm just an old fraud when it comes to anything like that." Then her voice firmed. "But I'd sure make him think I would. Believe you me."

"I still wouldn't want to get close to that cane of yours," Felicia told her, "even if you do say that you don't think you would use it."

With her hand on the outside door, Joan turned back. "Is there a back door here?" she asked. "I just remembered that guy saw us go in here. He might still be waiting for us to come out."

Claudia nodded and led them to a back door that led out into a little courtyard or playground surrounded by a high wall.

They had not realized it before, but during the afternoon, clouds had moved in to cover the sun. It had rained a little. The street was still wet. By now a thick fog was moving in, making the twilight hours as dark as midnight.

They crossed the courtyard, and Claudia opened the narrow gate to let them out into the alley. Felicia and Joan looked around uncertainly.

"I don't know whether this was such a good idea or not," Felicia said, trying to mask her uneasiness.

"Nonsense," Mrs. Halverson exclaimed. "I'm having more fun than I've ever had before."

She took Joan by the arm and started forward. "To tell you the truth," she concluded, "I'll be a little disappointed if our fat friend isn't hiding out here somewhere waiting."

"Mrs. Halverson!" Joan gasped. "Don't even think such a thing!"

Claudia led them down the narrow alley to a side street where she hailed the first taxi that went by and instructed the driver to take them back to their hotel.

"I had thought it would be nice if we could take you to the little cafe where we've been having dinner, Mrs. Halverson," Felicia said as they neared their destination, "but we've had a long day. I think it would probably be better to eat in the dining room in the hotel, don't you?"

The older woman nodded her agreement. "I hate to admit it," she answered, "but I think you're right. In fact, I wouldn't mind lying down for a few minutes before we go to eat. I'm more tired than I thought I was."

They left the cab and entered the hotel lobby. The door had scarcely closed behind them when the assistant manager came mincing out of his office.

"*Signora,*" he said, "and *Signorine,* I must ask a thousand pardons of you. Never in all the years that we have been operating the Hotel Metropole have we had this sort of thing happen."

Usually his English was impeccable, but now his consternation was so great his accent grew thick and difficult to understand.

A spasm of fear squeezed the breath from Felicia's lungs. Her eyes met Joan's. "W-w-what is it?" she managed.

"It is so embarrassing," he went on, his hands fluttering nervously. "I have never have anything like this happen before – and on my shift! Never will I be able to hold my head up again! It is terrible!"

"Young man!" Mrs. Halverson said sternly. "Just calm yourself and tell us what this is all about!"

By this time, his agitation had lessened somewhat. "While you are gone, someone break into the *Signorina's* room!" he exclaimed.

Felicia gasped aloud.

CHAPTER 6

A POLICE INVESTIGATION

For the space of a minute or two, silence held the tense little group like a vise. Felicia trembled, and for one terrifying instant, it seemed that she could not breathe.

"I am so sorry," the assistant manager repeated agonizingly. "I ask you a thousand pardons."

Joan wet her lips with the tip of her tongue. "Was anything stolen?"

"The police are making a search now," he said. "We call them right away – as soon as it happen!"

He rolled his eyes again and shook his head in disbelief.

"You caught them, of course?" Mrs. Halverson said.

He looked injured as he said, "*Signora,* it is the duty of the police to apprehend criminals in this country. As soon as the cleaning lady called down that she saw someone enter the girls' room, I have notify the proper authorities without delay."

The gray-haired woman's eyes widened. "You mean you didn't go up and catch them?" she echoed. "You didn't even try?"

"*Signora,*" he began once more, frostily. Her indignation made his composure complete once more. "The clerk at the desk was out for tea. I had no one available to care for the needs of our guests. At the Hotel Metropole, the rule is that someone be on duty at the desk at all times."

"In other words," she said, peering steadily at him, "you are too scared to go up there."

His cheeks paled. "*Signora,*" he said sadly, "you are being very unkind."

"You can stand down here and talk if you want to," Joan said, "but I'm going up and see what's been taken."

"Excellent suggestion," the assistant manager said, falling in beside her. "And when the manager talks with you about this tomorrow, will you so kindly tell him that I have offer my apologies – that I have do everything to give you the assistance. That you know I am not at fault?"

"Certainly," Felicia told him. "We don't blame you."

He seemed visibly relieved.

They made their way up the third flight of stairs and along the corridor to their room.

Police were inside, and so were two or three

agitated hotel workers. A number of guests crowded curiously about the door.

When he saw them, the assistant manager drew himself up haughtily. "One side, please," he ordered, "One side, please."

He went before them, making a path for the girls and Mrs. Halverson into their room. "These," he said to the police officer in charge, "are the unfortunate occupants of the room. *Signorine* Bailey and Cartright."

He paused, wrinkling his nose. "And *Signora* Halverson."

The officer, who spoke a little English, turned to Felicia. "The cleaning lady was in room next to yours," he said, "when she heard someone open your door with key and go inside. She went to tell you that she had not had time to finish your room but would do it in a few minutes. She opened the door, and when she saw a man inside, she screamed and ran around the corner. When she came back, the guy was gone."

The assistant manager turned to Mrs. Halverson triumphantly. "See, no opportunity for me to apprehend criminal. Already gone by time I was notified."

"But was anything stolen?" Joan broke in. "That's what I want to know."

"That is something we have wait to ask you."

They looked about hurriedly. "The suitcases are here," Felicia said moments later, "and the violin."

He made a notation. "That is good," he said, "very good. Nothing stolen."

The assistant manager brightened. "You may not know it," he said, turning to the girls, "but I have instruct cleaning ladies – all the employees – to keep a sharp watch for anything that might make inconvenience or unhappiness for our guests."

He drew himself up proudly and straightened the boutonniere in his lapel.

"I would not wish credit from one of lesser employees," he said, "but it is my alertness in anticipating possible trouble that saved you from loss."

He paused and coughed politely. "However, I suggest that you give valuables to me to be put in hotel safe for duration of your stay. No thief would tackle the staff of the Hotel Metropole twice. We must be sure we are doing all in our power to save you from embarrassment and loss."

The policeman was just finishing filling out his report.

"A petty thief," he said. "I'm confident that he has had such a good scare that he won't be back."

At last, the officer, having apologized for taking their time and causing annoyance, left. Joan closed the door behind him and locked it.

Mrs. Halverson dropped heavily to an overstuffed chair. "Now what do you make of all this?" she demanded.

"That's what I'd like to know," Felicia retorted.

"We don't have anything worth stealing. They ought to know that by seeing the way we're dressed."

"Maybe the thief thought he was getting into your room, Mrs. Halverson," Joan suggested.

But the older woman shook her head. "He couldn't. There hasn't been time enough for anyone to find out where I was staying. I only moved in here yesterday, you know."

Now the ticking of the cuckoo clock on the wall was the only sound in the small room.

"No," Mrs. Halverson continued, "there has to be some other reason. The thief wasn't after me. He was in the room he wanted to be in. I'm convinced of that."

"But you know that we don't have anything that anyone would want to steal," Joan said.

"The violin!" Felicia exclaimed. "That must be what he was after!"

Joan laughed dryly. "Come now. You can't make us believe that your new violin is worth so much someone wants to steal it. Olivetti let you have it for fifty dollars, remember?"

"But nobody followed us before we got it," Felicia countered.

"Well," Mrs. Halverson broke in, "quit fussing about it and get it out here so I can see it. You girls are beginning to get me excited."

Felicia got out the violin case and opened it. The gray-haired woman's eyes gleamed as she took the instrument in her hands and studied it carefully. The strings had been loosened, and the bridge was lying in the bottom of the fitted case.

"It's a rather pretty instrument, isn't it?" she asked.

"Fifty dollars' worth?" Joan asked, glancing in Felicia's direction.

"I suppose this is too weird to have a chance of being true," she said, "but do you suppose there could be something hidden in the violin – in the case?"

The girls frowned thoughtfully. "I don't know," Felicia said. "Where would a person start looking?"

"That's just it. We'd probably have to tear everything apart to look, and we still don't know what we're looking for or whether there was anything to find."

Joan noted the time. "Are we going to sit up here and look at one another until we starve to death," she asked, "or are we going down to dinner?"

Felicia took the violin from their guest, closed the case, and hid it in the back of the closet behind their clothes.

"I don't think anyone would dare to break in here again tonight," she said, "even if they are after the violin, but if we hide it, that ought to slow them down anyway."

They went down to the dining room after a few minutes. The service was no slower than usual, but Felicia chafed impatiently until they had finished and were ready to go back to their room again.

"You girls can do as you please," Mrs. Halverson said, turning her key in the lock, "but I'm going to bed."

Joan took her Bible and opened it to the place where they had been reading for devotions, but she did not read immediately. "What do you think about what has happened?" she asked.

Felicia did not have an opportunity to answer. The phone rang raucously.

The girls were both startled.

"A-a-answer it," Joan Bailey said.

"You answer it," Felicia countered. "It's probably just Mrs. Halverson wanting to tell us something."

"It wouldn't be. If she wanted to talk to us, she'd come in. She's right next door."

The phone rang again, and Felicia lifted the telephone. "Hello, Miss Cartright speaking." Her eyes widened, and her hand on the phone began to shake violently.

"What is it?" Joan demanded, leaning closer. "Who's on the line?"

"I–I–" she began. But the words caught in her throat.

Joan could hear the excited torrent of English and Italian that was being poured into the receiver. "Who is it?" Joan asked again. "What does he want?"

The phone went dead!

For a minute or two, Felicia held it in her trembling hand. Then, mechanically, she returned it to its cradle.

"Who was it?" Joan asked a third time, weakly.

"I–I don't know," Felicia answered. "All I could understand was that he said something about a violin!"

CHAPTER 7

AN INCONVENIENT ABSENCE

Joan Bailey grasped the edge of her chair in a quick, involuntary little gesture. Her gaze met Felicia's; fear answered fear.

"You don't think it was Mr. Olivetti?" she asked at last.

"It couldn't have been," Felicia answered slowly. "Mr. Olivetti spoke such good English that we both remarked about it. Whoever called me just now spoke so broken and talked so fast I couldn't understand what he was saying."

Joan reached over and touched the telephone with her index finger. "Isn't there anything else you could understand?" she asked hopefully. "Even a couple of words?"

"He said something about *Signorinas* Bailey and Cartright a couple of times," Felicia answered, "and *Signora* something-or-other. I suppose he meant Mrs.

Halverson. But those words and violin were the only things I could understand."

Joan breathed slowly. "Then this violin does have something to do with all this," she said.

"I've had the uneasy feeling that it has all along," Felicia told her.

"But what?" Joan questioned.

Her companion frowned. "That's something I just don't know."

There was a long, painful silence.

"Do you suppose the clerk at the desk would have any idea where the call came from?" Joan asked finally.

"You can't trace a call at home unless you have the cooperation of the telephone company and keep talking for quite a while." Felicia shook her head. "I don't think we've got a chance of finding out."

"Did the man sound threatening?" her roommate asked, "or did he sound as though he wanted to help us?"

Felicia went to the bathroom and got a drink of water. "While I was talking to him, I was so excited and upset I didn't think about anything," she said. "But now that you mention it, I just don't know. He was so upset and talking so fast and broken I couldn't make anything out of what he was saying. I couldn't tell whether he was friendly or not."

"I don't suppose it would do us any good if we did know," Joan went on. "There's nothing much we could do about it either way."

"We could go to the police," Felicia said, "but I don't know what we'd tell them if we did."

"Why don't we talk with Mrs. Halverson about it tomorrow?" Joan said. "She will be able to tell us what to do."

Felicia went to the closet and checked to be sure that the violin was still there.

The next morning when Mrs. Halverson came to go to breakfast with them, they told her about the phone call. Her eyes glinted with excitement.

"I knew it!" she exclaimed. "I knew it! When I heard your phone ring last night, I almost came in to see who it was and what had happened."

She lowered her voice. "And what are you going to do now?" she asked.

"That's what we wanted to ask you," Joan told her.

"Humph!" she snorted. "What would an old woman know about such goings on?" But she was obviously pleased that they had included her and were asking her advice. "Let me see. We could go to the police, I suppose, but unless we got an officer who could speak English, we might have a lot of trouble making him understand what we were talking about."

She got up and moved to another chair. "And we can't just ignore what's happened and pretend that it'll go away."

"Do you suppose your nephew, Mr. Turner, could help us?" Felicia asked.

Mrs. Halverson beamed. "That," she cried, "is a great idea! He'll be able to come up with something."

She paused. "He knows me well enough," she said sternly, "that he'd better come up with something!"

Her eyes were agleam, and excitement showed through in every movement.

"Now that that's settled," she went on, "suppose we go down and get breakfast so we don't keep Claudia waiting."

They got their coats and started to leave the room when Felicia stopped. "Do you suppose we dare to leave the violin here in the room today?" she asked. "Not after what happened last night, I'd say."

"We could put it in the hotel safe," Joan answered. "That is, if the safe is big enough."

"There won't be room for it," Mrs. Halverson said. "I saw it when I took my rings and a watch down to have them stored. Even if they took everything else out, I don't believe they'd be able to get that violin in."

"But if someone should break into the room again," Felicia said, "he'd get it for sure."

"Unless there was some real good place to keep it," Mrs. Halverson almost whispered. "Some place where they would never look."

Joan looked up. "That's it!" she exclaimed.

Felicia and Mrs. Halverson stared at her curiously. "What are you talking about?"

"We can ask the cleaning lady to put it in one of

the linen closets on this floor," Joan said. "No one would ever think of looking there."

"Do you think we could trust her?" Mrs. Halverson put in.

"She had a good honest face," Felicia said, "and she was the one who surprised the thief in our room. I'd almost bank on her being honest."

"Well," the older woman said, "there are times when we have to trust someone."

The cleaning woman wasn't on their floor when they were ready to go down to breakfast, so they hid the violin behind the shower curtain in the bathroom and went down to eat. When they came back, they sought her out and asked her if she would keep the violin for them.

"But certainly," she said. "I put it down here." She led them to a linen closet near the stairway. "I am the only one who has a key. It will be safe here."

She put the violin case in the back of the closet behind a stack of clean sheets and locked the door.

"I feel better about that now," Mrs. Halverson said. "It ought to be safe there until we talk with Dick and find out what he thinks."

On the stairs, she stopped and faced Felicia and Joan. "How much of all this do you think we ought to tell Claudia?" she asked.

"I don't know," Felicia said. "I hadn't even thought about it."

"Somehow I don't trust that girl as much as I'd

like to," the older woman said. "I think probably we had better be careful of what we tell her – for a while, at least."

In the lobby, Mrs. Halverson told their young Italian guide that she wanted to stop by the American Embassy. "I want to see that nephew of mine," she explained simply.

At the embassy, she took Felicia with her and told Joan and Claudia to wait outside. "We'll be back before you know it," she said.

She had intended the visit to the embassy to be short, but she had not expected it to be as short as it was.

"I'm sorry," the receptionist said when Mrs. Halverson asked for him. "Mr. Turner is out of the city and won't be back for several days."

"Now just what do you mean, he's out of the city?" she demanded curtly. "Just where did he go?"

"I'm sorry, but I'm not at liberty to disclose either his destination or the purpose of his trip."

Mrs. Halverson glared at her. "I'm his aunt."

"I'm very sorry. Is there anything else that we can do for you? Would you like to talk with someone else?"

Her scowl darkened. "No," she retorted. "No, thank you. We'll wait and talk with him when he gets back – if he ever does."

She took hold of Felicia's elbow. "Come, my dear."

CHAPTER 8

THE MUSEUM AND A SCARE

Joan saw that there was something wrong the minute Mrs. Halverson and Felicia came out of the embassy. It was written on their faces. They tried to act casual and unconcerned, but that was impossible.

"Well," Mrs. Halverson announced, "I guess we're ready to be on our way."

"I'll get a cab," Claudia said. "The places we are going today are too far to walk."

Joan moved toward her roommate. "Did you get to see Mr. Turner, Felicia?"

"He wasn't in," she answered. "And the way it sounded, he probably won't be back for several days."

Joan frowned seriously. "Now what are we going to do?" she asked guardedly.

"Wait, of course," Mrs. Halverson told her. "What else can we do?"

Felicia looked up to see Claudia staring at them, a

strange look on her youthful face. Mrs. Halverson's doubts about their guide came to Felicia at that moment, forcefully. Was she actually eavesdropping for a purpose or was she just curious? Or was she thinking of something else and not eavesdropping at all?

"The cab is here," Claudia said abruptly.

Joan followed Mrs. Halverson into the taxi, questions still racing unanswered in her mind.

Claudia Proveddi took them that morning to one of the large museums on the other side of Rome, a museum filled with artifacts that dated back to the time of the Caesars.

"You said that you have been interested in seeing the places where the Christians were persecuted," she told them. "These are the things that thrill me. Rome had everything that the world had to offer in those days – beautiful homes, parties, and excitement!"

Her eyes lit up as she talked.

"The Bible has a verse for that," Mrs. Halverson said. *"For what shall it profit a man, if he gain the whole world, and lose his own soul?* Rome gained the whole world of her day; the sin and materialism of her people caused her to fall."

Claudia's young body stiffened, and for a minute, she stood motionless, a scowl disfiguring her face. "We had better hurry," she said. "There is much to see in here."

They went into the museum and started down the long, wide corridors. Claudia knew the place well and told them story after story of the items they saw. It was intensely interesting.

They made their way through the west wing of the huge building and up the stairs to the second floor. Mrs. Halverson and Joan had moved ahead with Claudia, leaving Felicia a short distance behind. She was studying the English guidebook to the museum to learn the history of some of the jewels Claudia knew little about. It was all so interesting that for a time she completely forgot them – until she looked up into the swarthy, scarred face of a man who had been following them.

Felicia caught her breath. "Who are you?" she demanded hoarsely. "What do you want?"

The smile that twisted his evil-looking face did nothing to ease the dread that gripped her.

"Eduardo sent me to see you," he said guardedly. It seemed to Felicia that his eyes did not remain motionless but were constantly surveying the scene around them.

She looked desperately for Joan, but she, with the others, was out of sight. Muscles in her throat constricted, and her mind went numb.

"Eduardo?" she asked stupidly. "Do I know an Eduardo?"

"But yes. Eduardo Olivetti. The man who give you violin to keep for him."

Felicia gasped. That violin again!

"Eduardo got the money from his brother," the

man went on. "He couldn't come today, but he asked me to bring it to you and pick up the violin."

He moved closer, and for one brief, agonizing instant, she thought he was going to grab her. Involuntarily, she shrank away. He followed her until his dark face was close to hers.

"The violin," he repeated. There was just a trace of accent in his voice. "Eduardo wants me to give you the money and bring the violin to him. He say, 'Thank the young *Signorina,* but bring my beloved violin back to me.' I tell him that for a friend, I will do it. So, I have come for Eduardo's violin."

"But I–I don't have it here," she protested weakly.

His smile gave way to a dark, sinister scowl. "I have my car outside," he informed her. "It will only take short time to go to your hotel and get the violin."

He looked around again. "I have no time to waste. Hurry!" He reached out to take her by the arm, but she jerked away.

"If you're in a hurry," she replied evenly in spite of her own racing heart, "you'd just as well go now, because I'm not going with you."

Desperation grew. Where were Joan, Mrs. Halverson, and Claudia? Why had they gone on and left her?

The man's face grew livid, and anger kindled in his eyes, but for an instant, indecision seemed to grip him.

"Eduardo is not going to like it if I don't come back with violin," he said ominously. "It's going to make him awful mad. He'll come after it himself, and if he does, he's apt to get rough."

"If–if that's the way he wants to treat someone who helped him," she countered defiantly, "tell him to go ahead."

She started forward. "Now excuse me, I'm going to join my friends."

"You're coming with me!" he snarled. His hand snaked out suddenly and tightened on her wrist.

For an instant, Felicia almost cried out in pain. Then she remembered something they had been taught in one of the gym classes at Wellington. She grasped his wrist with her other hand and gave a sudden jerk. She caught him off balance and jerked him off his feet. He went sprawling into the heavy wood display case with such force that it staggered him.

"Joan!" Felicia screamed, dashing frantically down the aisle of the museum. "Mrs. Halverson!" Felicia's shrill cry went reverberating through the rooms of the museum.

She dashed around the corner, her shoes clacking a wild staccato to her cries. The very suddenness of her scream seemed to freeze guards and visitors. Even Joan, Mrs. Halverson, and Claudia stared as she came running to them.

"Joan!" she panted weakly. "Joan! Joan!" For the moment that was all she could say.

"What's the matter?" the Bailey girl demanded, seizing her by the shoulders.

"What's wrong, Felicia?" Mrs. Halverson asked, her voice rising.

"I–I–" But the words would not come.

By this time, someone, probably an officer of the museum guard, shouted a command, and the uniformed guards converged on her. So did half a hundred visitors of different nationalities.

"Young woman!" one of the guards who could speak a little English snapped. "We cannot permit such conduct in the museum."

"T-t-that man tried to grab me!" she protested. "He took hold of my arm!"

In spite of herself, Mrs. Halverson gasped, and Claudia's olive face went pale. The guard looked at Felicia in obvious disbelief.

"Such things do not happen in this museum, *Signorina,*" he told her coldly. "We do not permit it. I am sorry, but I am going to have to ask you and your friends to leave."

"B-b-but," she spluttered.

"You have already caused more disturbance than we like to have. Please go quietly."

Mrs. Halverson took Felicia by the arm and started down the aisle.

"Come, my dear," she said. "A Wellington girl never stays in a place where she's not wanted."

"But that man grabbed me!" Felicia protested. "I had to get away!"

One guard went before them and two guards behind to lead them to the nearest exit.

"You are welcome to come back," the guard said, the expression on his face unchanging, "when you can come to look in dignity and restraint."

Mrs. Halverson snorted indignation. "We shall never come back," she announced, "until the director of the museum himself comes to our hotel and apologizes to the girl."

Felicia breathed hard and slowly.

"I was so glad to get away from that man," she said, "that I don't even care what else happened."

"What man?" Joan asked.

Felicia looked around, as though half expecting to see him approaching them. "The man who has been following us," she whispered.

Claudia was trembling, too. "Do–do you want to do any more sightseeing today?" she asked, "or–or has this made you want to stop for the day?"

Mrs. Halverson glanced at Felicia and Joan. "I don't know about you two," she said, "but I can't see that we're going to be able to change things any by going back to the hotel and folding our hands."

"You'd like to go on, then?" She nodded crisply.

"As soon as we get something to eat, I'd like to go on." She turned to Felicia. "But first I've got to find out something about this man who grabbed you. What did he say, Felicia? What did he want?"

"He was after the violin."

Mrs. Halverson straightened. "I knew it. I knew it the first time we laid eyes on him that that was what he was after."

"He said he is a friend of Eduardo Olivetti and was going to pick up the violin for him."

Briefly she told them what had taken place and how she had thrown the squat, little man to the floor and gotten away from him.

Laughter played in Mrs. Halverson's eyes, and her smile broadened. "I'd give most anything to have seen that, Felicia," she exclaimed.

Joan snickered. "I'll bet he was surprised."

"As I always say," Mrs. Halverson went on, "a Wellington girl can take care of herself in almost any situation."

"I don't know about that," Joan countered. "Felicia didn't do so well when it came to keeping us from being kicked out of the museum."

Only Claudia Proveddi said nothing about what had happened. She took a step or two to one side and looked up and down the street. "There should be a good place to eat close by," she said finally. "If you don't mind walking a block or two."

"You lead the way," Mrs. Halverson directed. "We'll follow you." She went up and walked beside their young guide.

"What do you make of what happened just now, Felicia?" Joan asked in low tones.

"There was something strange about it that I didn't think of until just now. That man didn't follow us into the museum. He was waiting there for us just as though he knew we were coming."

Joan glanced up at Claudia significantly. "You know, this is the first morning that we haven't decided where we wanted to go ourselves."

"That's right. Claudia told us that she wanted to take us to the museum this morning."

"And I thought she acted a little disturbed when we told her we wanted to go by the American Embassy on the way here." There was a brief silence. "Do you suppose she knew that guy was waiting for us?"

Felicia took a deep breath. "I'd hate to think that she did, but we're going to have to keep a close watch on her," she said. "You know, Mrs. Halverson had a hunch that we couldn't entirely trust her, and she's not often wrong about people."

"We'll have to be careful what we tell her from now on."

Mrs. Halverson looked back at them impatiently. "Are you girls going to hurry," she asked, "or are you going to let me starve to death right here on the sidewalk?"

Felicia and Joan hurried to catch up with them.

"We're sorry," Joan said, "but in talking, we forgot that we ought to be keeping up."

Claudia's eyes met theirs. It was almost as though she knew what they were talking about.

"I'm awfully sorry about what happened back at the museum," she said. "In a way I feel responsible. I was the one who insisted that we go there this morning."

CHAPTER 9

CHANGE OF LOCATION, BUT PROBLEM STAYS

They went into the cafe and sat down.

"I'm hungry," Joan said, picking up the menu and staring at it. "I wish I could read this thing, so I'd know what I was ordering."

"You liked the 'little hots' Mama served yesterday," Claudia said, consulting the menu. "They have those."

"That sounds very good to me."

Once they had finished ordering, Mrs. Halverson fished in her copious purse and pulled out a couple of booklets. "I had these in my room, Claudia," she said. "I think your father would like to read them. Would you take them to him?"

Claudia looked at the titles. "How to Know God," she said, translating from Italian into English. "The Joy of the Christian Faith."

She opened the booklets and glanced through them.

"You might enjoy reading them, too," Mrs. Halverson continued. "Especially the one about joy and happiness. Those are two things that most young people are interested in."

"Joy?" Claudia's lower lip curled to reveal her bitterness. "There isn't any such thing unless you have lots of money and can get everything you want. I don't think I'll ever know what it is."

The older woman laid a hand on Claudia's firm young arm. "I have lots of money," she said with a simplicity that showed she wasn't boasting. "I can buy anything I want to buy. I can go anywhere I want to go and do what I want to do. But, my dear, I found a long time ago that I couldn't buy happiness. True happiness, I have found, is a gift of God and comes only through serving Him."

"You can say that money doesn't mean anything," their guide countered, "because you have all you need or can ever hope to need."

"My mom doesn't have much money, Claudia," Felicia put in. "The only reason I can go to Wellington School is because I got a large scholarship that pays most of my expenses. I've found that what Mrs. Halverson says is true. The only real happiness I've ever had came after I confessed my sin and put my trust in Christ."

"I think that's the thing that makes a Christian happy," Joan said. "The knowledge that the penalty of our sins is paid for, once and for all, and knowing we have met God's conditions and are going to heaven makes happiness. The person who has trusted Christ has something to base happiness on."

Claudia's eyes darkened, and she looked down at her plate. She picked up her fork with trembling fingers and laid it down. "That might be all right for some people," she retorted, "but it's not for me."

The waitress came and set bowls of soup before them. When she left and after they had bowed their heads to ask the blessing silently, Felicia continued.

"The Bible tells us that salvation is for everyone who will receive it, *For God so loved the world, that he gave his only begotten Son, that whosoever believeth in him should not perish, but have everlasting life*."

Claudia Proveddi flinched. "You just don't understand," she whispered. "You don't understand."

"I wish you'd let us help you," Felicia told her gently.

Their guide's eyes met hers, blazing furiously. "Leave me alone! Please!"

"I'm sorry, Claudia, I certainly didn't intend to offend you."

Claudia was quiet and reserved the balance of the afternoon. They went to another museum and to several churches near the center of Rome. Shortly after five o'clock, she excused herself and went home.

"I'll be able to stay a little longer tomorrow night," she said, "but something has come up that makes it necessary for me to go a little early this evening."

"That's quite all right," Mrs. Halverson told her. "We'll see you in the morning."

She started away but turned back. "And thank you for the books," she said. "Thank you very much. I know that Papa will enjoy reading them."

When she was gone, Mrs. Halverson led the girls into a nearby restaurant for a cup of tea. "Now," she said, leaning forward and lowering her voice when they had been served, "what are we going to do?"

Felicia and Joan studied the situation quietly. "About the violin?" Felicia asked her.

"And the little, fat man you threw into the display case," Mrs. Halverson went on.

"I hope we don't have to do anything more about him." The Cartright girl shuddered. "I get goose bumps just thinking about him."

"He probably gets more than that from thinking about you," Joan said, laughing.

"We're not through with that guy yet," Mrs. Halverson continued, "unless I'm badly mistaken. He wanted that violin badly and followed us around, then tried to talk you into turning it over to him. He's going to be back."

Felicia was really shaken visibly. "W-what are we going to do?" she asked.

"That's something we've got to work out," the gray-haired woman said. "And we've got to do it before dark. He won't dare come around before then."

"Don't you think the violin is safe right where it

is?" Joan put in. "No one is going to think of looking in that linen closet."

"I'm not sure it is," Mrs. Halverson said. "No one would think about it being in there, but what if that cleaning lady gets to talking to someone? She might let it slip that she's taking care of it."

"That's right," Felicia replied. "But we've got to do something with it. We can't keep it in our room."

She shivered, then added, "I'm not even sure that I want to stay in that hotel any longer after all that's happened."

"Why don't we change hotels?" Joan asked. "If we could slip away now before anyone starts following us again, we might be able to get completely away, at least until Mr. Turner gets home."

Mrs. Halverson toyed with her spoon for a moment. "You might have something there at that," she said.

"If Claudia isn't in league with them and giving them information," Felicia put in. "If that's happening, it won't do us any good to change hotels."

"That would be one way of finding out if she is on their side," Joan Bailey said. "If the guy started following us right away, we'd know that she was giving him information about us."

"But that still doesn't solve what we're going to do with the violin," Felicia whispered. "I don't think it would be safe in our room even if we did change hotels."

"Does the bus depot and the railway station have

parcel lockers like they do back in the States?" Joan asked in a hushed voice.

Her companions both nodded.

"I saw them when we came in from Switzerland last week," Felicia said.

"If we could sneak the violin into one of those, we could hide the key somewhere and be sure no one would find it," Joan suggested.

Mrs. Halverson smiled brightly. "A wonderful idea, Joan!" she exclaimed. "I'm glad you're a Christian and on the side of the law. If you were a criminal, all of these ideas of yours would make you terribly hard to catch."

"Dad always did say he thought there was a little fraud in me," she answered.

They paid their check and went back to the hotel where they sought out the cleaning lady. She had finished her work for the day and was just going out the side entrance on her way home when Joan and Felicia caught up with her and asked for the violin.

"Yes," she said in broken English, "I have the violin safe, but I–I thought you were going to leave it with me for time."

"We were," Felicia said, "but there has been a change in plans."

The cleaning woman went back to the third floor and got the violin case from the linen closet for them. Mrs. Halverson tipped her liberally.

"Thank you," she said, "but I would have been glad to have kept it for you."

They took the case into their room and locked the door. Joan checked the case to be sure that the violin was still in it.

"Now, how are we going to get it to the depot without being seen?" the gray-haired woman asked uneasily. "A person is slightly conspicuous with a violin under her arm."

"Too bad Felicia doesn't have a moustache," Joan said, laughing. "We could dress her up in a tuxedo, and everyone would think she played in a symphony orchestra."

Joan crossed to the window and came back again. "We don't have to leave the violin in its case," she said. "Wouldn't it fit in your suitcase?"

"I suppose it would," she answered reluctantly, "but what would I do with my clothes?"

"We can worry about that later."

"You can talk," Felicia countered. "They're my clothes."

"You were the one who got us into this mess in the first place by loaning this Eduardo Olivetti fifty dollars," Joan said. "Remember?"

Felicia went to the closet and got the suitcase. It was just large enough for the violin.

"There!" Joan said, closing the bag. "That's taken care of. Now they'll not know the violin is anywhere within miles."

"I still would like to know what I'm going to do with my clothes?"

"You can cram a few into one of my suitcases," Joan told her, "and some more in yours. The rest of them you ought to be able to get into the violin case."

Felicia looked out. "It's raining hard now," she said. "We'll get soaked going to the railway station."

"Maybe we could have the bellhop take care of it for us," Joan suggested.

But Mrs. Halverson would not hear of it.

"No, sir," she said, "I don't think we ought to let this suitcase out of our sight until we put it in one of those lockers and turn the key. We don't know who we can trust and who we can't."

"I suppose you're right," Joan went on, "but I sure hate to go out in all this rain."

"The more rain the better," Felicia put in. "That will make it just that much more difficult for our friend to follow us."

The girls got into their raincoats and took the suitcase to the railway station. Mrs. Halverson insisted on going along, but they would not have it.

"There's no need of you getting out in this wet and cold," Felicia told her. "We'll be back in half an hour and then we'll have to move to another hotel."

"Well, all right," she said reluctantly, "if you insist. You'll have to tell me everything that happens. Every single, solitary thing."

They made the trip to the railway station and

deposited the suitcase without incident. Thirty minutes later they were back in the hotel. Mrs. Halverson had her bags packed and was ready to go.

Felicia had a little trouble getting her clothes into the remaining suitcases. She put several good sweaters and skirts into the violin case, together with two pairs of shoes. The rest of her things she crammed into her other suitcase and into Joan's.

"I don't know why I let you talk me into things like this, Joan," she grumbled good-naturedly.

"Because it's the only sensible thing to do."

Felicia stopped suddenly and straightened.

"You know, there's one thing we haven't thought of," she said. "If Eduardo Olivetti comes for his violin in person, how is he going to be able to find where we are if we change hotels?"

"We could leave a note for him at the desk telling him where we are," Joan said.

"But if we did that," Mrs. Halverson put in, "someone who claimed to be Eduardo Olivetti could ask for the note and find out where we are. Or someone in the hotel might be tempted to open it and read it."

"But the violin belongs to him," Felicia said. "I'll have to make some sort of arrangements for getting in touch with him."

Joan thought for a moment. "I know what we can do," she said at last. "We can leave a note telling him to get in touch with Mr. Turner at the American Embassy. That way the right man can find us, and we won't have to worry about anyone else knowing where we are."

Mrs. Halverson had already gone to the desk and was writing the note.

Once that was accomplished, they gathered their bags and went downstairs. The assistant manager who had been on duty at the time of the attempted robbery a few days before was on duty. He was disturbed to see them leave.

"I do hope that your decision had nothing to do with the unfortunate occurrence of a few days ago," he said.

"Not entirely," Mrs. Halverson told him, paying the bill.

"And where will you be staying?" he asked pointedly.

The older woman's gaze met his, evenly. "We won't need help with our bags," she said. "We can manage them."

"But what shall we do with your mail?" he insisted – a little too forcibly, it seemed to Felicia. "And your phone calls? What will be your new Rome address?"

"Why don't you send the mail and phone calls to the American Embassy in care of Richard Turner?" she suggested. "He will know where to get in touch with us."

"And," Felicia said, "if Eduardo Olivetti should ask for us, would you please give him this note?"

"Eduardo Olivetti." He wrote it on the outside

of the envelope. "We shall see that he gets it. I will handle it personally, *Signorina*."

He smiled ingratiatingly and clapped for a bellboy.

"We will carry our own luggage," Mrs. Halverson told him.

They waited just inside the door while the door-man called a cab and helped them out to it. Mrs. Halverson started to protest once more, but he ignored her completely and carried her bag to the taxi. He put the bigger ones in the trunk, but Felicia kept the violin case in her hand.

They crawled into the cab and were just ready to announce their destination to the driver when the door opened suddenly on the street side and an evil, scarred face peered in.

"So!" the voice snarled in almost perfect English. "We meet again!" Before anyone could speak, he climbed in and pulled the door shut after him.

CHAPTER 10

THE BEST PLACE FOR THE KEY

Time stood still!

Felicia Cartright could not tear her gaze away from the man's evil face. He was wearing a raincoat and a cap that all but covered his eyes. There was no mistaking that he was the same man who had followed them and had accosted her earlier in the museum.

"You!" she gasped.

"Me! I told you that I'd be back! You should have come with me this morning, *Signorina*. You would have save yourself the much trouble."

"W-w-what do you want?" she asked weakly.

"Eduardo, he send me for his violin," he said. "This time I get."

He reached down and his hand closed over the violin case handle.

The driver, who had been waiting for someone to

tell him where to take them, half turned in the seat and spoke in Italian.

"Driver!" Felicia shouted. "He's trying to kidnap us! He's forced his way into the cab and is going to–"

Their unwanted guest spoke to the driver who turned back and started the engine.

The little man laughed. "You don't think it is that easy to get away from Alessandro, do you?" he asked. "That driver doesn't speak English. I told him that you had just remarked that it's raining hard tonight and you're glad that you don't have to walk."

He spoke once more to the driver and the taxi began to move.

"Where were you going at this time of night?" he asked. "Were you try to run away from Alessandro? Were you try to keep from giving him the violin?"

"You seem to know all the answers," Joan said, "suppose you answer."

As the cab inched out into the line of traffic, Joan reached for the door handle with a sudden movement. She intended to jump out and dash for help. But their captor's snakelike eyes saw her. His hand snapped out to grasp her wrist with iron fingers.

"I wouldn't try that if I were you," he snarled.

She settled back in the seat slowly, her breath tearing at her lungs and her heart hammering a fierce beat against her ribs.

"This morning I try to be good to you," he

continued. "I come to the museum, and I talk nice with you. I try to reason. And how you treat me!"

He rubbed his forehead with two fingers, tenderly. "It is a wonder you did not crack open my head."

"You got just what you deserved," Mrs. Halverson told him. "Any man who would try to make a poor, defenseless girl go with him deserves to get his head cracked open."

"Poor, defenseless girl?" he echoed. "As defenseless as a tiger."

In spite of their predicament, Mrs. Halverson permitted herself a faint smile.

"If I have any more trouble with any of you," he warned, "I'll forget that you are ladies."

The gray-haired woman's eyes flashed, and her lips formed a thin, straight line. "Young man!" she exploded, glaring straight into his eyes, "I am a patient, long-suffering woman. But if you lay a finger on either of these girls – if you so much as touch one of them – you'll have to answer to me personally. Do you understand?"

She thrust her chin up to his, and it seemed to Felicia that he flinched slightly.

"Now, if you know what's good for you, you'll stop this nonsense and have the driver stop this cab and let us out of here before I lose my temper."

For the space of a minute or two their eyes fought.

"I'll have you know that we are American citizens,"

Mrs. Halverson continued, "and we're not used to being shoved around."

"I have no need of you," he blustered at last. "All I want is the violin."

Mrs. Halverson snorted. "Well, you're not going to get it!"

"Just try and stop me!" He spoke to the driver who pulled over to the curb and opened the door. "Now get out of here before I change my mind!"

"Not until we get our luggage!" Mrs. Halverson retorted haughtily.

"But Mrs. Halverson!" Felicia pleaded, taking her by the arm.

She shook off the girl. "I don't propose to let a half-pint hoodlum get away with our luggage!" she repeated.

"You'd better do as the girl says, lady!"

"Don't you 'lady' me!" She shook her finger in his face. "If I were a man, I'd–I'd–I'd tweak your nose!"

The driver had gotten out of the taxi, gone around to the trunk and set the suitcases on the sidewalk.

As the driver came back to the cab and got in, Alessandro realized what he had done. "Your luggage is on the sidewalk, lady! Now please get out of here!"

He gave her a shove that almost sent her sprawling.

Felicia tried to hang on to the violin case as she scrambled out of the taxi after Mrs. Halverson, but the wiry little thief jerked it from her grasp.

He must have shouted to the driver at the same

instant, because the cab began to pull away even before Joan got out; she almost fell before Felicia caught her.

They remained motionless, the rain dropping on their faces. Their gaze followed the cab through the maze of traffic until it turned two or three blocks up the street and disappeared.

Mrs. Halverson pulled her raincoat tightly about her throat and buttoned the top button.

"That man!" she exploded. "I've never been so furious at anyone in my life! Imagine treating us that way! His mother certainly didn't teach him manners when he was growing up!"

Felicia turned back to their suitcases. "We'd better get another taxi and get out of here!" she exclaimed. "I don't want to be standing on this street when he finds that the violin isn't in that case!"

She caught her breath. "Joan!" she wailed. "Do you know what has happened? My clothes! My best sweaters and skirts!"

The Bailey girl only laughed.

"Joan, it was your idea!" Felicia continued. "It's your fault! You're going to have to get them back for me. That's all there is to it!"

Mrs. Halverson waved down a cab and gave the driver the address of the hotel near the Proveddi apartment.

"You know," she said, chuckling, "our little, fat man is certainly going to be surprised when he opens that violin case and finds that he has only got a couple of skirts and three wool sweaters. I'd like to see the look on his face."

"You know what's going to happen, don't you?" Joan said. "He's going to tear Rome apart looking for us. And when he finds us–" She shivered.

"Rome's a big city," Mrs. Halverson said.

"But he hasn't had any trouble finding us so far," Joan replied.

The older woman sighed. "That's only too true," she said. "And I'm afraid he's had past help in locating us."

The taxi stopped before the door of the small hotel, and the driver set their suitcases on the curb. A bellboy came and helped them.

The hotel was smaller and not quite as nice as the one they had just left, but it was clean and the man at the desk was friendly. Like the desk man in the other hotel, he also could speak English fairly well.

"Yes," he told Mrs. Halverson, "we have a safe for the valuables of our guests. If you will bring them down, we will put them in the safe and give you a receipt for them."

Up in their hotel room, Felicia looked at Mrs. Halverson and Joan. "We've got to find some safe place to put this key," she said, taking the locker key from her pocket and looking at it. "If anyone looking for the violin found this, they would know for sure what it is and have a good idea what is in it."

"We don't dare to carry it with us," Joan said, "and I don't suppose we'd dare to hide it in the room."

"That would be almost as bad as keeping the violin here," Mrs. Halverson agreed.

"But what are we going to do with it?" Felicia asked before she answered her own question. "I have it! Joan, where's that little jewelry box of yours?"

"Now that is too obvious a place," she answered. "That's just about the first place they'd look."

"But we're not going to leave it here," Felicia countered. "We're going to take it down to the hotel safe and have them keep it for us."

She removed a small drawer from the jewelry case, taped the key securely to the bottom, and returned it to its place. "Now no one will ever know where it is," she said.

Felicia took the box down to the desk at the same time Mrs. Halverson took her rings. The receipt she placed in the toe of her shoe. "Now, that's taken care of," she said, breathing deeply. "We ought to be able to get some sleep tonight."

CHAPTER 11

THE HAPPIEST DAY OF ALL

The following morning, Mrs. Halverson got the girls up an hour earlier than usual and hurried them to breakfast.

"We've got to get around this morning," she said. "We've got to be over at the Proveddi apartment before Claudia leaves for the other hotel, or she won't know where to find us."

"Maybe that wouldn't be such a bad idea," Joan put in.

"I suppose you have a reason for saying that," the older woman said.

"I was just thinking about Claudia and wondering if she is actually the one who told the man where we were going and where we stayed. If she is the guilty one, then it might not be such a bad idea for us to stay here in the hotel for a few days – until your nephew gets back, Mrs. Halverson – not let anyone know where we are."

"I don't know about that," Mrs. Halverson murmured. "What do you think, Felicia?"

"We don't have any real evidence that Claudia is in with that man. In fact, she helped us to get away from him the other day if that means anything."

Joan was disturbed. "I know all of that, but it seems strange to me that he would be able to know where we were going to be and what we would be doing almost any hour of the day. And you said yourself that you didn't think he had followed us to the museum yesterday morning. You said you thought it looked as though he had been waiting for us."

"He could have followed us until he saw where we were going," she said, "and then parked his car and beat us into the building."

Mrs. Halverson set down her coffee cup. "I'm not in favor of hiding from a little pip squeak like him," she said. "We came here to see Rome. I say let's see Rome! And just let him dare try to annoy us! Just let him dare!"

Felicia smiled and so did Joan.

When they finished breakfast, they went to the Proveddi apartment and rang the doorbell. Claudia's face lit up when she saw them.

"Oh, there you are!" she exclaimed. "Come in, won't you?" She showed them into the living room. "I've been so concerned about you."

Felicia's eyes narrowed. "What do you mean?"

"You had checked out of the hotel," the girl explained, "and I didn't know where you had gone. I tried to phone Mr. Turner, but he's gone too."

Mrs. Halverson sat down heavily. Her gaze found Claudia's. "Just how did you learn we had checked out of the hotel?" she demanded testily. "Who told you that?"

Claudia flushed. Before she could answer, Papa and Mama Proveddi came in. As soon as they saw Mrs. Halverson and the girls, they smiled broadly and came over to shake hands with them.

Then Papa turned to his daughter and spoke to her.

"It was because of Papa," she began in English after a moment or two, "that we tried to get in touch with you last night. He started to read those books you gave him."

Felicia's pulse quickened. "Did he have questions?" she asked.

"Yes," Claudia replied cryptically. "He had some questions."

Her father pulled up a chair and sat down before he spoke again.

"He says it is hard to understand how a person can be saved without working for it," his daughter interpreted. "How can he be saved and go to heaven without doing good?"

Mrs. Halverson straightened and looked directly at him. "The Bible says *the wages of sin is death; but the gift of God is eternal life through Jesus Christ our Lord.*"

She paused while Claudia translated for him. "We don't work for a gift," she said moments later. "Someone makes us a present of it."

She reached over for one of the books she had given him which was lying on a table not far away. "I gave this book to you yesterday. You didn't work for me and earn it."

He nodded understanding.

"So it is with eternal life. Because we are so wicked and want our own way so much, we could not possibly do enough to earn salvation. The Bible tells us that even the smallest sin is enough to keep us out of heaven, where God, who is holy, dwells. God loved us so much that He sent His Son to die on the cross for our sins and be raised again so that we might be saved."

Felicia prayed silently as Mrs. Halverson continued to talk with Papa Proveddi about Christ and what was necessary to become a Christian.

Claudia found great difficulty in looking into Mrs. Halverson's eyes.

"Tell your father that salvation is for everyone – whether they have committed big or little sins. God's love for us is so great that He makes it possible for all to be saved."

Claudia's lips parted and she tried to speak, but she could not. She looked at Mrs. Halverson and the girls in desperation then leaped to her feet and fled from the room. Her father and mother stared after her helplessly.

The girls sat there, staring at one another. Mr. Proveddi motioned for one of them to go into the bedroom after her. At first, they did not understand, but he went through the motions again.

"I think he wants us to go in and talk with her," Felicia said, getting to her feet. "Come on, Joan."

As they stood, her father smiled and nodded vigorously, pointing to the bedroom door once more.

They found Claudia lying across the bed, sobbing uncontrollably. Joan and Felicia got on either side of her.

"Claudia," Felicia said, touching her on the shoulder. "Claudia."

The young woman did not move.

"Claudia," Joan whispered, "you can be saved too. Salvation is for anyone who will put his complete trust in Christ as Savior. Confess that you are a sinner and trust Him to save you."

"It's not for me," she said at last. "Not after what I've done."

"Christ told the thief on the cross that he would be saved," Felicia added.

There was a long, painful silence.

Claudia rolled over and sat up, rubbing her tear-stained eyes uncertainly with the back of her wrist.

"It's really a good sign when you feel that you're

not good enough to be saved," Felicia told her gently. "I think that is the one thing that keeps more people from becoming Christians than anything else. Most who aren't Christians feel they're so good that they don't have to be saved."

The girl on the bed started to cry again. "But you don't know what I've done," she wailed. "You don't know what I've done."

She squared her shoulders and took a long, deep breath. "I–I told Alessandro where you were staying," she blurted. "I took you to the museum and got the others away from you, Felicia, then he came to talk to you."

Joan and Felicia looked at one another briefly.

"We're not too surprised," Joan said. "We suspected it had to be that way."

"You–you mean that you knew?" she asked incredulously. "You still were nice to me?"

"We weren't entirely sure," Felicia said, "but it did seem that you were about the only one who could have been telling him – either that or he was being awfully lucky. Almost every time we turned around, he was there."

"He–he told me that you had his brother's violin and wouldn't give it back," she said. "He said that all he wanted to do was find out where you were and what you were doing so he could stop you if you tried to sell it."

Tears escaped from under her eyelids and trickled down her cheek.

"That didn't seem so bad to me," Claudia continued. "I–I was so anxious to get things that I–I would do almost anything for money."

"Don't worry about it now," Felicia said. "We understand."

Their guide had difficulty in speaking. "You are so different than anyone else I've ever known," she said at last. "You make me want to be like you."

"No," Felicia countered, "don't say that. The important thing is to be like Christ."

Starting at the beginning, Felicia and Joan outlined the plan of salvation. Using one Bible verse after another, they pointed out how a person had to recognize his lost condition and that Christ had the power to save.

"The Bible tells us," Joan concluded, "that God will never reject those who come to Him."

It was only a few minutes before they knelt with Claudia and she accepted Christ as her personal Savior.

When they finally came out of the bedroom, Mrs. Halverson had no need to ask what had happened. Claudia's face was radiant.

She spoke to her parents in Italian. It wasn't long until they, too, knelt and asked Christ to come into their hearts. Mrs. Halverson, Felicia, and Joan explained more of the truth of the gospel to them with Claudia's assistance as an interpreter so they would be sure to understand.

"Well, now," the gray-haired American said when they got to their feet. "This is a wonderful day. I don't know when I've been so happy."

Claudia related that to her father and mother, who beamed broadly.

They had planned to go sightseeing, but instead, they spent the entire day in the Proveddi apartment going over the Scriptures together and explaining the most important truths of God to the new believers. It was difficult having everything translated – difficult and very slow. And before they quite realized it, the day was gone.

"I'll talk with my nephew," Mrs. Halverson said as they rose to go, "and find the name and address of the pastor of a Bible-believing church and have him call on you. Now that you know the Lord, you will need the fellowship of other Christians to grow as you should."

They got their coats and Claudia went down the elevator with them. "I want to go and eat with you," she said. "There is so much I'd like to talk with you about – so many things that I don't know."

They were so excited about Claudia and her parents accepting Christ that they forgot completely about the violin, Alessandro, and Eduardo Olivetti until they stepped out onto the street in front of the apartment house. Three men slipped out of the darkness and surrounded them.

"Now don't make a move!" a familiar voice rasped.

"Alessandro!" Claudia exclaimed.

"Alessandro! You have double-cross me, Claudia! You were to have American friends in the Catacombs this afternoon!"

He turned his attention to Felicia. "You make sport with Alessandro!" he rasped. "That I not like!" As his anger increased, so did his accent. "I tell you not to fool with Alessandro! Not to make with the lie."

"Nobody lied to you," Mrs. Halverson broke in defiantly. "And if you are going to talk to Felicia and Claudia, you keep a civil tongue in your head. Do you hear?"

He spat on the walk contemptuously. "I'm taking care this! I'll do as I please, and you are not going to stop me!"

Mrs. Halverson, who was carrying her cane, brought it down resoundingly on his toe.

"Ow-w-w!" he yelled.

"Run, girls!" she shouted.

But the other men grabbed them roughly before they had an opportunity to move.

"Oh, no, you don't!"

CHAPTER 12

AN EXCITING NIGHT

For the last time I warn you!" Alessandro raged. "You do that again, *Signora,* and I–I'll–" His voice died away threateningly.

"You had just as well know it now," Mrs. Halverson said defiantly, "I'll do it any time I like."

"Take that club away!" Alessandro ordered.

She jerked it back and stared from one to another hotly. "You leave this cane of mine alone!" she ordered. "If you don't, I'm apt to forget I'm a lady." She drew the cane back menacingly and stood her ground. The men made no move to disarm her.

"Come on," Alessandro ordered, "we've got to get on our way." He grabbed Felicia by the arm and shoved her ahead of him to their waiting car. "Now get in there," he snarled, "and don't give us any more trouble, or we'll get rough!"

They shoved Mrs. Halverson and Felicia into one car and Joan and Claudia into another.

"Young man," the gray-haired woman asked imperiously, "where are you taking us?"

He did not reply.

The driver turned and drove along a section of the old Roman wall, through a gate, and to the outskirts of the city. Felicia tried to look for landmarks as they sped along, for anything that might give them a clue to their location and where they were heading. The driver turned so many corners and drove so fast that she soon realized it was useless.

She glanced at Mrs. Halverson, who had her eyes closed and was moving her lips silently. Just knowing that the older woman was praying was a help. She prayed too.

"Do you suppose they'll take Joan and Claudia to the same place they're taking us?" Felicia asked after several minutes.

Mrs. Halverson shook her head. "I don't know," she whispered, "but I'd imagine they'll keep us together – at least until they find out where the violin is."

"Why do you suppose they're taking us way out here?" Felicia wanted to know. "They know that we haven't been so far away from the hotel since we got to Rome. The violin couldn't be out here."

"I've been wondering about that myself," Mrs. Halverson said. She ran her hand over her forehead, and Felicia saw that she was trembling.

Finally, the driver switched off the lights and

wheeled the car through a huge gate where he braked to a stop. Only then did Felicia and her companion see that there was another car behind them.

"God answered our prayers," she whispered to Mrs. Halverson.

"All right now," Alessandro said in a hoarse whisper. "Get out of the car and step lively. We haven't got all night."

"I'm not used to being ordered around," the gray-haired American said irritably. "That sort of talk is going to get you nowhere with me."

Nevertheless, she got out of the car and followed Felicia up a narrow, twisting walk to the side entrance of a huge villa that was entirely dark. Joan and Claudia were right behind them.

"Just where are you taking us?" Mrs. Halverson demanded loudly.

"You'll find out," their captor told her. "Now get along with you and keep your mouth shut."

The men herded the three girls and the older woman into a large room which must have been a library or drawing room. It was completely dark. Alessandro checked to be sure the drapes were tightly closed. Then he struck a match and lit the candles in the candelabra. The dim yellow light revealed a row of bookshelves along one wall and a number of pieces of very old furniture scattered about on the thick Persian rug.

"All right," Alessandro said suddenly, "where is that violin?"

"You'll not find out from me!" Mrs. Halverson snapped.

He glared at her. "Maybe I won't!" he exclaimed. "But I know a way of finding out."

He directed his attention to Felicia and Joan. "If you don't want me to get rough with your gray-haired friend, you'll tell me what you did with that violin!"

"Don't tell him!" Mrs. Halverson ordered. "I'm not afraid of him."

"You might not be afraid of me now, but you soon will be, I'll guarantee. If we don't get that violin pronto, I'll show you whether you have to be afraid."

"What I can't figure out," Joan said to him, "is why everyone is so excited about that violin. Felicia only loaned Eduardo Olivetti fifty dollars on it. It surely can't be worth any more than that."

"A genuine Stradivarius only worth fifty dollars?" he asked. "That is to laugh! That violin is worth over a million dollars! What's more, I intend to have it!"

Felicia and Joan stared at him stupidly.

"A Stradivarius!" Joan murmured under her breath.

"But I don't get it," Felicia countered. "If it's actually a Stradivarius violin, why would Mr. Olivetti give it to us as security for a fifty-dollar loan?"

Alessandro laughed. "That just proves how cunning Eduardo is. He stole the violin but couldn't risk keeping it himself because the police were on his trail. A relative of his who works at the hospital told him about you girls, and he cooked up that scheme to get you to keep it for him until after the police – and I – quit trying to find it."

Felicia's eyes widened. "You–you mean that he used us to keep stolen property for him?" she asked in disbelief.

"You were used, all right," he answered.

"But where is he? If he's the thief, why isn't he here now to–to get his violin? Or why didn't he come after it himself? All that he needed to do would be to ask for it. We'd have given it to him."

"It seems that Eduardo is in jail," Alessandro said, grinning. "Somebody called the police and tipped them off about some of the smuggling and thievery Eduardo has done, so they came and took him out of circulation."

He moved closer. "I have taken care of getting Eduardo out of the way. Now I am taking over on the violin. Where is it?"

"We're not going to tell you," Felicia said defiantly. "That violin is going to the police."

"Is it in your hotel room?"

She remained silent.

"Did you give it to someone to keep for you?"

Still, she did not reply.

He reached out and took hold of her purse. "Maybe there is some clue in here."

She relaxed her hold on her purse and felt her gaze being drawn, irresistibly, down to her shoes where she had placed the hotel receipt. Alessandro noticed something in the look on her face.

He dropped his hold on her purse. "So!" he said triumphantly. "You have some clue in your shoe!"

The Cartright girl cried out and tried to jerk away.

"So it is the shoe!" His voice rose, and he grabbed her roughly by the arm. "I tell you Alessandro will find! This is better! This is more better!"

"Alessandro!" one of the men warned. "Keep your voice down!" He must have been an American because he spoke English without a trace of accent. "Keep your voice down. My cousin is caretaker here, and he said we could use the villa tonight, but the police go by regularly. If they hear us, pouf!"

While this was going on, Joan edged over to the library table where the lighted candelabra was and leaned back until her hands could touch its base.

Alessandro was on his knees by this time. He had pulled off one of Felicia's shoes and then the other. His fingers trembled with greed as they reached frantically into the toes.

Mrs. Halverson nodded significantly and took a firm grip on her cane with both hands. "Now!"

Joan turned the candelabra over and jammed it hard against the table. The candles broke and snuffed out.

Felicia, who hadn't realized until that instant what was happening, kicked out with her foot, catching Alessandro in the face and sending him sprawling with a cry of rage.

Mrs. Halverson had taken a tight grip on her cane and measured the distance to the other two men very accurately. She swung her cane twice, and each blow brought a howl of pain.

All was confusion in the big drawing room. The two men were yelling at the girls and at one another. Alessandro was scrambling around on the floor in the darkness trying to find Felicia's shoes.

"Come this way!" Claudia Proveddi shouted above the noise. She flung open the door and stopped short, blinded by the beam of a police flashlight.

"So!" the officer exclaimed in Italian. "What goes on here?"

* * *

At the railway station an hour later, an English-speaking officer went with the girls to open the locker. The owner of the valuable instrument went along.

"That is it!" he cried in a voice that carried over all the station. "My violin! My beloved violin!" He grasped Joan by the shoulders suddenly and startled her as he kissed her on both cheeks. "You have bring back my violin!" he said again, tears filling his eyes.

He turned to Mrs. Halverson as though to kiss her, too, but she retreated a step or two and raised her cane.

"Oh, no, you don't!" she warned. "Not as long as I have this cane."

On their way back to the hotel, the officer told them how Eduardo Olivetti had almost succeeded in getting away with the violin.

"Or I should say Alessandro," he went on. "Eduardo's plan was ingenious in that we would never have thought to link you girls with him. We arrested him and searched everywhere we could think of for the violin – even searching the homes of his friends and acquaintances. That is how Alessandro first found out about it and stepped in to try and get it for himself."

He paused while they crossed the narrow street.

"If the officer on duty hadn't seen the light in the villa drawing room and gone to investigate, Alessandro might just have gotten away with it."

"Light?" Felicia echoed. "What light?"

"When Alessandro and his friends pulled the drapes, they weren't drawn tightly. That was very fortunate for us."

"Fortunate, young man?" Mrs. Halverson echoed. "I'll have you know that *I opened those drapes with my cane.*"

He left them in the lobby of the hotel. "You will come down to the station and identify Alessandro and his companions tomorrow?" he asked.

"It won't take long, will it?" Mrs. Halverson asked. "There are a lot of things to see in Rome. We want to do and see what there is."

She glanced at the girls. "I don't want these girls, Felicia and Joan, going back to Wellington and complaining that their stay here was dull and uninteresting."

THE
FELICIA CARTRIGHT
SERIES

Felicia Cartright, a petite blonde who is one of the most popular students at Wellington School for Girls, has a surprising inclination toward mysteries. If a mysterious situation arises, it either makes its way to Felicia, or Felicia somehow finds it. Though this is a bit trying for her happy-go-lucky roommate, Joan Bailey, it does prevent life from becoming monotonous. It also enables Bernard Palmer, the popular author of the "Danny Orlis" books, to write an entertaining series of stories for girls aged twelve to eighteen.

The mysteries range from a valuable missing antique to an attempt by claim jumpers to steal a deposit of tungsten ore. There's excitement and action galore—but there's also spiritual guidance and blessing because Felicia and her partner-in-adventure love the Lord and take Him into account in all their experiences.

AVAILABLE FROM WWW.ANEKOPRESS.COM